A blessing to follow

D1390301

A blessing to follow

Contemporary parables for living

Tom Gordon

WILD GOOSE PUBLICATIONS

To
Alexander William Day,
my first grandchild,
whose birth has been an inspiration,
and to whom I hope I can tell many, many stories.

Contents

Preface

The Gaels have a word for 'storyteller': *seanachaidh*. It refers to the bard who passes on a community tradition and makes it live again … and again. I remember one particular storyteller from the Hebrides – the late Attie McKechnie, who lived on Mull, and took part in the rebuilding of the living quarters of Iona Abbey. His stories about the restorative work on the walls – with (sometimes inept) divinity students acting as labourers for the craftsmen – were both funny and instructive. And his tales drawn from the pool of Hebridean mythology were magical. With that musical accent of his, he drew you spellbound into a world which was both natural and almost supernatural.

George Fielden MacLeod, founder of the Iona Community, was also a *seanachaidh*. He told stories, and told them again and again – so much so that members of the Iona Community could recite them, word for word. Indeed, members would make affectionate fun of George, mimicking the stories and emphasising the punchlines. He would tell the same tales so often that members of his own family would cry for mercy. Yet the great Celtic spellbinder knew exactly what he was doing: nearly two decades on from his death, his community still knows the stories. Orkney's bard, George Mackay Brown, was another *seanachaidh*. Much influenced by the Icelandic sagas, GMB saw at least part of his vocation as being the retrieving and retelling of tales from Orkney's ancient and more recent past.

Jesus Christ was a storyteller. He didn't preach long sermons – many biblical scholars believe that the Sermon on the Mount was a compilation of teachings made at different times and places – but his stories stay in the imagination of believers and non-believers alike. There are subversive tales about farmers and housewives and fishermen and tax collectors and prostitutes; and who could forget stories like the Good Samaritan and the Prodigal Son? Jesus himself was the inheritor of stories which were repeated at the camp fires of Israel – Adam and Eve, the Exodus from Egypt, Joshua and the Walls of Jericho, David and Goliath, Solomon's legendary wisdom, Jonah and the whale, and so on.

Now Tom Gordon will be more than a little surprised to be named in such illustrious company, but he is a natural storyteller whose gift is to see the transcendent in the ordinary and express it in vivid contemporary terms. He stands in a long tradition of bards in the Jewish and Christian traditions. Tom confesses that he doesn't know how a story emerges. 'It just seems to be "out there" and it's my job to catch it and write it down,' he says. 'I've never been too bothered about how it happens, but I'm happy that it does.'

His stories aren't about farmers and rabbis – familiar figures in the biblical landscapes – but about gangs and footballers and hospice patients and so-called 'sink' housing estates. He sees the activities of God in these tales, but he expresses the insights without lecturing or moralising. Like all good storytellers, his stories carry a power which needs no tedious elaboration.

There are stories here about a poor boy who has to share his shoes with his dad, 'dossers' who live on the streets, an inscription on a park bench, a woman standing at the grave of the love of her life, the return of a soldier from Iraq, a creaking gate near a graveyard, the battered face and brain of a boxer, a pair of red dancing shoes, graffiti on a church wall, wedding china, a cat in a crematorium, a boy called Elvis, and lots more.

There is one particularly moving story – the only one told by Tom in the first person. Josie, a patient in the hospice at which Tom was chaplain, asked for a communion service before she went back home. A bit irritated because he had so much to do, Tom agreed, but in a rush he brought the wrong book. He tried to bluff his way through the communion service, but Josie had a surprise for him, one which blurred the distinction between celebrant and participant. How? Well you'll have to read the story.

This book is a helpful resource for both personal devotion and public worship. In fact, it is structured around the Christian year, a framing which is appropriate for the material. As well as stories there are lectionary readings, prayers and poems. But above all, the ancient and contemporary power of stories to move, to instruct, to comfort and to inspire is affirmed and celebrated.

Ron Ferguson

Introduction

I've always enjoyed telling stories - to entertain family and friends; to anchor images and characters for ever in the memory; to prick a bubble of stress or confusion; to allow a situation to have its own life without the need for explanation; to help illuminate complicated ideas and concepts. But, above all, telling stories is fun, enjoyable in the telling and in the reactions of the hearers.

Over the years a number of stories have remained in my memory bank, along with fragments of ideas which deserved to have a story built around them to bring them to life. So a question kept coming up: 'Of what lasting use are such stories?' Such a purpose has begun to become clear.

It began at funerals. The more I offered contemporary readings alongside scripture, the more people commented on the relevance and the helpfulness of the images and insights created. Then there were opportunities to share stories in worship, with children and with adults, where a story could stand for itself and not need an additional explanation. This continued in the writing of *A Need for Living* and *New Journeys Now Begin*, where stories were at the core of the lessons and insights shared. And when I was asked by others to write stories for use in their anthologies of worship and reflective material, a specific style of storytelling began to emerge. In addition, friends and colleagues talked of the need for a 'contemporary lesson' in worship, to stand alongside traditional readings. And, indeed, some have collected such lessons and written their own.

The final piece of the jigsaw was a casual conversation with Janet Jackson, a colleague in hospice chaplaincy. She spoke of weekly worship in the hospice and the problem of finding something that was short, relevant and helpful in that context. 'We need a book of stories,' she said.

This book, therefore, is a product of all of that. It is a collection of stories with several uses: in worship, as contemporary lessons or sermon illustrations; in small-group settings as stand-alone stories that need no explanation or conclusion added; to be read for personal reflection or thoughtfulness; to be told to others as an offering of insight or support.

The next question was, 'How might these stories come together in one place?' There were a number of ways I could have done that, but I've chosen as a framework for these stories *The Revised Common Lectionary*. Given the date of publication of this book, the stories will follow Year 3 of the Lectionary, from the beginning of the Christian Year in Advent through to the following November. I hope that this will be followed by companion books for Years 1 and 2 of the Lectionary. Consequently, there are fifty-two stories, one for each Sunday, with some additional stories to cover Holy Week and other additional special days.

This, of course, is a Christian pattern, because that is what I've lived with all my life, the linking of ideas and celebrations, events and special seasons in an unfolding of a story of hope, meaning, purpose and fulfilment as the year goes by. So the framework I've chosen comes from what I know, and the familiarity of it helps me make sense of the developing drama of the human condition.

But the Lectionary is simply a framework, providing a guide to the issues of our living, and, therefore, the themes of the stories themselves. I hope that this chosen framework is not off-putting to those who are not familiar or not comfortable with Christian ideas and patterns. For there are deep meanings and common insights for the whole of humanity to which we can be directed through what we know and are familiar with. These stories will transcend one tradition or pattern, for they are designed to have their own life and meaning and to be accessible to all. They work without the need for any guiding system. We are all human and need to stop and think from time to time about what really matters. These stories help us do that.

Many of the stories will benefit from being read aloud. And that doesn't mean they can only be read aloud in worship, or with a small group, or in a sermon, or to inform other people. Try reading them aloud for yourself. They work well that way.

There's only one story in the book, 'Beyond words', which is told in the first person. And there's only one story, 'Beauty from the ashes', which is based around a recognisable incident in recent memory and which names one of the people involved. I'm grateful, therefore, to John Weir Cook and David Innes for their permission to tell this story and to publish the poem which I wrote for them at the time – offered here in a slightly revised form. All the other stories are about anonymous people.

Of course, the themes of some of the stories have their birth in actual events, in my own experience or as told to me by others, but they have been recreated in a completely fictional context. Many have their beginning in an idea or a thought, a story blossoming from a small seed, to become something new and different from anything else. All contain fictitious characters and situations, and any similarity to any people or places familiar to you is purely coincidental.

I've written one story around a saint's day – St Andrew's Day, November 30th. St Patrick, St George and St David will be for other books, but for now I'm happy to have a Scottish bias, for Scotland is the country of my birth - as well as the country of the dialects in some of the stories which I can hear in my head as I am writing them down.

I don't quite know how a story emerges. It just seems to be 'out there' and it's my job to catch it and write it down. I've never been too bothered about how it happens, but I'm happy that it does. I attended a big conference a couple of years ago. One of the speakers was deadly dull, and I found myself idly gazing around the room. I spotted a lady on the far side of the conference hall who was wearing the most extraordinary red shoes I had ever seen, quite out of keeping with the sober dress of the other conference participants and even of the wearer of the shoes herself. I began to jot down some thoughts, transfixed as I was by this amazing footwear. A story slowly evolved. The result was 'Velda's shoes'.

I am grateful to John Birrell, Brian Embleton, Janet Jackson, Mark Primrose, George Sweeney and Alice Thomson for permission to make use of their ideas or events familiar to them as the basis for some of the stories. I can only hope that I have done justice to the context and meaning of their insights.

For her patience, feedback and encouragement, I owe a great debt of gratitude to my wife, Mary, who has laughed and cried at some of the stories I've read to her, and who, I hope, will laugh and cry at some more. And, of course, as she did for my first two books, she has taken the photograph for the cover of this one. That means a great deal to me.

I'm grateful to my family – Mairi for her enthusiasm for the project, James for his quiet reassurance, and Kathryn for her valuable feedback on aspects of child development and how children respond to things.

The manuscript for this book was completed during a stay on the Island of Mull, and I'm indebted to John Morrison for the use of his house in an environment so conducive to thoughtfulness, beauty and wonder, and an inspiring place in which to write.

There are many people – like the lady in the conference with the amazing red shoes - who, unknowingly, have given me the beginning of a story. They'll never know who they are, but without them some of these stories would never have seen the light of day.

Neil Paynter at Wild Goose Publications has been as affirmative and encouraging as anyone could possibly be. 'I like the way you write,' he said in an e-mail to me several years ago. He then invited me to write some short stories for *The Coracle*, the journal of the Iona

Community. Feedback from these stories has been both enabling and uplifting. To Sandra Kramer and all the staff at Wild Goose I offer my immense thanks.

I will be eternally grateful to Ron Ferguson for reading the manuscript and for agreeing to offer a preface. I can think of no greater privilege than to be affirmed as an author by a critically acclaimed writer.

The title of this book comes from a Scottish ballad. I've always enjoyed reading 'story-poems' and hearing a tale unfold as a ballad is sung. The poem 'Geordie's Marriage' by William Finlayson is such a tale, recounting in vivid terms the events and characters of a Highland wedding celebration. Part of the poem gives us this scene:

> *Sae the Fiddler he lilted an' play'd,*
> *An' the young anes I wat werena idle;*
> *While the Auld Bodies tippled, an' prayed*
> *For a blessing to follow this bridal.*

So now it's back to work to prepare two companion volumes, with my own prayer that there will be a blessing to follow in them, but with enough blessing to follow from now.

1 Anticipation

For a small boy in a small town the anticipation was almost too much to bear. It began with a banner strung across the main street, proclaiming in bold letters – as it did every year – 'Agricultural Show and Summer Fair, Town Park, First Saturday in July'. That was the start of it, and, in the weeks that followed, the increase in anticipation for a small boy was matched only by the escalation of preparations.

A huge marquee went up in the park where one set of football goalposts had been, soon to be followed in the last days of June by a proliferation of smaller tents scattered from one end of the park to the other. Indeed, as the great day approached, the area was transformed into a veritable tented village.

Bunting went up the week before the event, strung from the windows of the upper stories of many of the houses in the town down to their garden gates; festooned across the main street from the top of one lamppost to the top of another; looped along the fence which separated the town park from the road … millions of miles of colourful bunting, it seemed to a small boy, guiding the enquiring traveller right through the town, along the main street to the gates of the park itself, with the bunting continuing round the perimeter like a welcoming garland.

With a day to go, huge loudspeakers were erected on giant posts at all four corners of the park, and big men leaning out from a high cradle made sure they pointed in the right direction. 'One, two … one, two …, one, two, three … testing, testing … one, two …' would boom out mysteriously as sound-systems were tried out.

Wooden gates and pens were put in place for the Noah's ark of animals which would fill them in the early hours of the special day – cattle, sheep, pigs, horses, and always the family of goats from the farm across the loch. Big, colourful signs were fixed on poles outside the tents in anticipation of what would be available inside their canvas walls – 'Home-baking', 'Shepherd's crooks and wooden crafts', 'Knitted goods', and of course, by a canvas emporium a good deal bigger than the rest, the inevitable 'Beer tent'.

For a small boy in a small town, it all was almost too much to bear, as excitement lifted with the bunting, expectation increased with every new development and change, and anticipation rose with every sign of the Big Day's approach.

When the great day arrived, following a sleepless night for organisers, animals, and one little boy among many, many others, the Town's Annual Agricultural Show and Summer Fair never, ever disappointed. The expectancy was always the forerunner of something special. And, every year, the event surpassed expectations. For a small boy in a small town the anticipation was almost too much to bear. But it was well worth it.

Was it the same for a farmer with his prize sheep or best Highland cow? Was the same pleasure experienced by the family who brought their goats from the other side of the loch? Was the excitement shared by Mrs McDougall with her Victoria sponge and cheese scones, whether she won or not? Was a small boy's big sister just as excited with her knitted dolls and baby clothes? Was the anticipation too much to bear for the organising committee? You bet it was!

For a small boy in a small town the anticipation was almost too much to bear. But then again, it made the great day all the more worth the wait.

God of our Advent

God of our Advent,
the banner has been strung across the main street
of our journey of life and faith –
'Christmas is coming – only a few weeks to go.'
For our Advent has begun –

now it's preparation time;
now it's excitement time;
now it's time for childlike anticipation.

God of our Advent,
help us with our preparation
so that all will be properly ready for the great day.
Help us with our organising
so that together we might do what's right.
Help us with our attitude
so that our anticipation might almost be too hard to bear.

God of our Advent,
when the tented village of Christmas is ready
to offer once more
the fun,
and colour,
and precious exhibits
for all the people,
let my anticipation have done its job
when the great day arrives.

God of our Advent,
the Incarnation will come ...
and the anticipation of this Advent Season
will be worth it,
even though at times it will be almost too hard to bear.

First in Advent

Old Testament: Jeremiah 33:14-16
Epistle: 1 Thessalonians 3:9-13
Gospel: Luke 21:25-36

2 Angus gets ready

Long before the days of supermarket chains and out-of-town shopping malls, Angus McPherson sold fruit and veg from his horse-drawn cart. Angus was a ken-speckled figure around the villages along the edge of the loch, always attracting his familiar customers and small groups of excited children. For the customers, it was the quality of the produce that kept them coming, a fine mixture of the vegetables Angus grew in his kitchen-garden and the fruit and veg delivered to the rail-head in the local town. For the children, it was the horse ... for Atlas, Angus's ancient black-and-white steed, was always a favourite. Angus McPherson was a popular man.

Then there was the gossip ... for Angus was always the enthusiastic conveyer of this or that piece of local information. 'Did you know that Jessie Cameron's girl has fallen pregnant, and not yet married either? ...'; 'Fancy new car the minister has ... must be paying him too well ...'; 'I've heard tell the local bus is only to run twice a day and not three times ...'; 'Old Jimmy's failing fast ... not long for this world ...' Angus McPherson, purveyor of fine fruit and veg - and juicy pieces of local knowledge – was indeed a popular man.

New Year was always a great time for Angus and Atlas. Actually, it was a good time for Angus, for Atlas had to do most of the work. For with a dram or two at regular intervals, and more gossip exchanged than vegetables sold, Angus was usually in a pretty sorry - or happy - state by the time his round was over. That's where Atlas had to do his bit, for he knew the way well and would take himself home safely at the end of the day, stopping in the yard inside the farm gate. And there was Angus, slumped over the reins, only rousing from his slumbers with the bumping of the cart over the yard's cobbles.

But it was at Christmas time that Angus excelled himself. Not that there was much fruit and veg available over the winter months, and, with the shorter days, the visits to the villages were curtailed too. But there was still gossip and information to be purveyed, and the cart was always full of that! So Angus and Atlas's visits were as welcome as ever. And no more so than in the few weeks before Christmas when Angus transformed his cart into a thing of wonder and delight.

It began when he appeared with a string of golden, cardboard angels pinned all around his cart - the same angels every year, for as far back as people could remember. 'Why've you got these on your cart, Angus?' some curious child was bound to enquire. 'Because angels are messengers,' Angus would reply, 'and we're getting a message too.' And the children would gather round, and Angus would tell them stories – of angels and messages, and Elizabeth and Mary, and dreams and visions.

A week later he appeared in the village with the angels round his cart *and* a lantern hanging from a pole at the back – a storm lantern, the kind the villagers were all too familiar with as their precaution against the variability of the local version of the National Grid. 'Why've you got that lamp on your cart, Angus?' one of the children would inevitably ask. 'Because there's a Light coming soon for the whole world,' Angus would reply. And the children would gather round, and Angus would tell them stories – of lights and darkness, of lamps and pathways, of stars and stables.

Another week would pass, and he would come to the village again, with the angels round his cart, and the storm-lantern shining at the back, *and* Atlas would be decked out with a coloured rug across his back and a fetching straw hat over his ears. 'Why've you dressed up your horse, Angus?' would be this week's question. 'Because there's a gift coming, a special gift, and it has to be carried in a special way.' And the children would gather round, and Angus would tell them stories – of gifts and travellers, of donkeys and camels, of preciousness and anticipation.

But the best week of all was when Angus arrived with angels

round his cart, and a lantern on the back, and a horse all dressed up – *and* a few old apple boxes on the back of his cart. 'What's in the boxes, Angus?' excited children would ask. Angus didn't disappoint. For in the boxes there was a present for every child, a simple, home-made gift, created by Angus himself. 'Remember the best gift of all,' Angus would tell them as his gifts were distributed. And the children would gather round, and Angus would tell them stories – of mangers and babies, of shepherds and kings, of a Saviour and Christmas.

Angus McPherson, purveyor of fine fruit and veg, and local knowledge, and stories for children, *and* Good News for everyone. No wonder he was a popular man around the villages along the edge of the loch, and no more so than in those few weeks as Christmas itself approached.

Look!

Look, listen, wait, get ready –
for I bring you a hand-full of stories,
of angels and messages,
of Elizabeth and Mary,
of dreams and visions.

God of my looking,
help me look well for your coming.

Look, listen, wait, get ready –
for I bring you a box-full of stories,
of lights and darkness,
of lamps and pathways,
of stars and stables.

God of my listening,
help me to listen well for your coming.

Look, listen, wait, get ready –
for I bring you a cart-full of stories,
of gifts and travellers,
of donkeys and camels,
of preciousness and anticipation.

God of my waiting,
help me to wait well for your coming.

Look, listen, wait, get ready –
for I bring you a Life full of stories,
of mangers and babies,
of shepherds and kings,
of a Saviour and Christmas.

God of my readiness,
help me to be ready for your coming.

Second in Advent

Old Testament: Malachi 3:1-4.
Epistle: Philippians 1:3-11
Gospel: Luke 3:1-6

3 Prepared

When the Town Council decided that the old bandstand in the park was to be demolished and replaced with a new one, there were no complaints from the local people. The old bandstand had been an eyesore for years, and now, in its crumbling state, was a danger to anyone who ventured near. For some months a high fence had surrounded it, with red signs boldly announcing 'Do Not Enter', 'Danger', 'Keep Out' as warnings to all and sundry. But when the demolition had been agreed, the first thing to appear all the way around the park, enclosing the bandstand and everything else within the park boundary, was a high wooden wall. 'Temporary,' the Council had announced. 'To allow the work to proceed without interruption,' ran the story in the local paper.

All of this was lost on Gertrude. All *she* knew was that the whole park was out of bounds, a big, wooden wall barring her way to the sand-pit and her favourite swing-park. It even meant that she and mum had to walk the dog on the narrow strip of grass along the road, rather than allowing him to have the free run of the park.

One day, when Gertrude and mum were skirting the wooden enclosure on their way home from walking the dog, Gertrude asked, 'Mummy, what does "pro-se-cu-ted" mean?' 'Prosecuted?' her mum replied. 'Now, whatever put that in your mind?' 'There was a poster on the wall that said "pro-se-cu-ted", and I didn't know what it meant.' 'Oh, "prosecuted" … that'll be a warning to people to keep out of the park and if they don't they'll be prosecuted … That means they're breaking the law, and the police can arrest them, and they can go to court and be fined, or something like that. Does that make sense?' 'Yes, mummy,' said Gertrude. 'But it didn't say *everyone* will be prosecuted. Only Bill.' 'Bill?' Gertrude's mother responded, a puzzled frown appearing on her face. 'Who on earth is Bill?' 'Mister Stickers, mummy. Didn't you see? Look, there's another sign over there. Not everyone, only Bill. See?'

Gertrude pointed excitedly. And, sure enough, there on the wooden panelling, in bold, red letters, was the announcement, 'BILL STICKERS WILL BE PROSECUTED'. Gertrude's mum laughed out loud. Gertrude didn't see what was funny – especially when Mr Stickers was being singled out for this dramatic warning and no one else. Mum explained it all on the way home, and, of course, Gertrude now felt very silly indeed, her embarrassment complete when mum told dad the story after he got home from work, and they had both laughed for ages and ages.

But what Gertrude did now fully understand, was that sticking posters on the Council's wooden walls round the park was a *very* serious offence indeed – for everyone … And if you did, being prosecuted would surely follow.

That's why Gertrude was *extremely* surprised when, some weeks later, on her way home from school with her mum, she saw a workman fixing a large poster to the wooden wall at the corner of the park. 'Mummy, mummy,' that man'll be pro-se-cu-ted if he sticks that up there. He'll really be in trouble, mummy.' Gertrude's mum smiled. 'He's a Council workman, my love, and he can do what he likes with his own wall.'

The workman turned and saw the two ladies, and, having overheard their conversation, smiled at them both. 'Just wait till you see what the poster says,' he suggested, winking as he did so. And so, as they were bid, mother and daughter stood and watched while the Council workman fixed his big poster to the wooden wall. Satisfied, he stood back, and all three of them admired his handiwork. GRAND OPENING, the poster proclaimed. A SPECIAL BRASS BAND RECITAL TO CELEBRATE THE OPENING OF THE NEW TOWN BANDSTAND. And there followed details of the day and time of the great event, and what the band was to be, and who would cut the ribbon, and all the rest.

'You see,' said the workman, 'the work's about finished. It's been a long haul, but we're almost there. Only two weeks to go. We're just getting the final things done, and then there'll be the finishing touches. So we have to prepare you all for what's to come, to tell you we're nearly ready. We hope you'll come along. It'll be a great day. So our posters are to invite you all to a celebration that's just about here.'

Gertrude's mum thanked the workman and left him to his task of fixing posters all around the park. 'I'm glad we're getting our park back, mummy,' Gertrude announced as they were wending their way home. 'It's been *such* a long time. Can we go to the concert and hear the band?' 'Of course, my love, of course,' her mum replied. There was a long silence, broken only by Gertrude affirming, 'I'm glad the workman wasn't in trouble, mummy. Because if *he'd* been Bill Stickers and been arrested then we wouldn't know everything was ready, would we?' And her mum nodded and smiled wisely.

Ready

Ready to go when the day has arrived;
Ready to join the event;
Ready to share in the frolics and fun;
Ready to state my intent.

Ready to come to the party at last;
Ready to join with the throng;
Ready to share when the crowds are in place;
Ready to feel I belong.

Ready to know that the time has come round;
Ready to join with the praise;
Ready to share with the band striking up;
Ready in wonder to gaze.

Ready to find out the worth of it all;
Ready to join with the rest;
Ready to share in the laughter and song;
Ready, prepared for the best!

Third in Advent

Old Testament: Zephaniah 3:14-20
Epistle: Philippians 4:4-7
Gospel: Luke 3:7-18

4 The best Christmas ever

Ernie and Mags were particularly proud of their house at Christmas time. Before the days of people lighting up their houses and garages and roofs and gardens like Blackpool illuminations, Ernie and Mags were operating at a *much* lower level. It was a string of fairy lights in the window, and a couple of coloured bulbs liberated from the Council Christmas tree in the park to create a romantic soft-light effect in the hallway that did the trick.

But there was one year when Ernie and Mags were struggling even more than usual. Money was tight, and the thing they missed the most this particular Christmas was a Christmas tree. 'It'll not be a proper Christmas without a tree,' Ernie moaned one day when he met the local priest outside the post office. Sadly, Father Gallagher wasn't able to help, and had to say so, leaving Ernie and Mags to a treeless Christmas.

Until, that is, Father Gallagher got a phone call from one of the secretaries at the city Seminary. The students had gone home for holidays and there was a Christmas tree in the foyer which would have to be thrown out ... unless someone could take it 'for a needy family to brighten up their Christmas'. Father Gallagher jumped at the offer, and he knew *exactly* which family was going to benefit from this kind gift. But the trouble was transportation ... The Community Centre mini-buses were all booked out, and, try as he would, he just couldn't access other transport. Time was against him. The Seminary was about to close. Ernie, Mags and the kids weren't going to get their tree after all. Unless ...

'I'll collect it in my car,' the resourceful priest pronounced to himself. 'So what if it sticks out the window a bit? It isn't a long drive, and I'm sure the local police will turn a blind eye if I'm stopped ... and I've got my dog-collar on ...'

So that's why Father Michael Gallagher was pondering tree-into-car logistics in the quadrangle of the Seminary later that day. And the logistics weren't great. For a start, the tree was *much* bigger than he had been led to believe. There was nothing else for it ... The tree would have to be tied to the roof-rack. So, that's why the College secretary and a red-faced priest were lugging a monstrosity of a Christmas tree onto the roof-rack of a Mini Traveller when one of Father Gallagher's former theological teachers happened along. 'That tree on that roof-rack?' he politely enquired. 'Needy family,' Father Gallagher replied. 'And anyway,' the secretary chimed in, 'we've had the tree sprayed with that stuff that means the needles don't fall off on your carpet. Holds them on like super-glue, my mum says.'

Now, this was either a good sales-pitch or was offered with forcefulness in case the local priest changed his mind and decided not to take the tree after all. In any case, the theologian simply offered a quizzical 'Mmmm', which seemed to be the only suitable response at the time.

So, a theologian goes about his business, a secretary feels good that a Christmas tree is going off to a needy family, and a priest, with a large tree now firmly attached to the roof-rack of his Mini-Traveller, heads off to brighten the Christmas of Ernie, Mags and the kids.

Now ... this was when a trusting Father Gallagher began to doubt the sales-pitch of a Seminary secretary's mum re the effectiveness of the 'stuff you spray on to make sure the pine-needles don't fall on your carpet'. Or maybe it's that the effectiveness is OK if the pine needles aren't subjected to the wind they experience on top of a car in an ever-increasing winter gale. Either way, he began to realise that, even if the pine-needles were individually stapled to their branches, there was no way these needles were going to stay in place on the journey home.

The car behind him at the traffic lights turning a delicate shade of green gave the game away. And it was the bus following him with its wipers on when it wasn't raining that made him realise he might have a problem. And when he pulled up ten minutes later in front of *Chez Ernie & Mags*, there was not one solitary needle left on the tree. There were deflated balloons, some old tinsel, and one surviving bauble, but no green pine-needles. The tree was absolutely bare.

But when Ernie and Mags came running out of their stair, they were as excited as little kids on Christmas morning. 'Father,' Mags cried, 'ye've brought a tree. God, an' the kids'll be right chuffed. This'll be the best Christmas ever!' Pretty soon Ernie was installing the brown arboreal skeleton in the corner of the front room. It's amazing what you can do with some coloured crepe-paper and more balloons and tinsel, though. And, soon enough, the tree was … well … better! Not great, but better. And Ernie, Mags and three fascinated kids had their Christmas tree after all.

Early in the New Year Father Gallagher bumped into the erst-while theological teacher who'd been so sceptical on the day of the tree's collection from the Seminary. 'How did you get on with that tree you were taking to the parish before Christmas?' he enquired with a wry grin. 'Mmmm,' Father Gallagher replied - which, he reck-oned, was the only suitable response at the time …

The best Christmas

It's the best Christmas ever
when someone gets a gift
beyond their wild imaginings and dreams.
It's the best Christmas ever,
when expectations shift,
and spirit-songs have hope among their themes.

It's the best Christmas ever -
the Gift above all else
is offered now from Love's own treasure-store.

It's the best Christmas ever
as Grace comes down for all,
to fill our homes, to bless our lives once more.

Fourth in Advent

Old Testament: Micah 5:2-5*a*
Epistle: Hebrews 10:5-10
Gospel: Luke 1:39-55

5 The Nativity Play

It began without any great fuss. The Nativity Play in the local school had followed the same pattern for generations. It took place in the school hall, and there was an open invitation to parents and visiting dignitaries to come along. Parents and others sat in rows in the back half of the hall. Facing them, making three sides of an open square, sat the well-scrubbed and wide-eyed 5- and 6-year-olds from the Primary 1 and most of the Primary 2 classes. The selected youngsters from the chosen P2 class for that year who were the 'principals' in the nativity drama were safely ensconced in the gym changing room.

The Christmas story unfolded along familiar lines. The children sang a Bethlehem-type song, and in from the changing room, encouraged by a fraught P2 teacher, came the beaming Joseph and adorable Mary, bedecked respectively in striped tea-towel tied round the head with dad's old tie, and a blue veil, which looked suspiciously like the same material as the curtains in the upper-school staff loo. Despite Joseph's passion for waving at his mum in the back row - and the silly woman waving back – and Mary's veil slipping dangerously over her eyes, the expectant couple arrived safely at the stable, right in the middle of the open square of carolling children.

The innkeeper got his words right – no funny stories to tell of fluffed lines this year - the baby Jesus was duly delivered and laid in the manger, and the shepherds made their entry complete with crooks and stuffed animals under their arms. (Well, there was *one* animal that did look like a lamb, but what was that lad at the back doing carrying a monkey with red and white striped trousers? Oh well, the value of modern exegetical interpretation of scripture ...) The tableau was almost complete, Mary and Joseph centre stage, shepherds watching their menagerie on Bethlehem's plains by night, and the angelic P1 and P2s singing beautifully.

All was ready for the entry of the three kings. The pianist belted out the appropriate chord. The choristers struck up with an impressive kingly song. The changing-room door opened, and in walked – *two* kings. 'We three kings from Orient are …' with one who seemed to have got lost along the way. The two kings, however, appeared to have no knowledge of their wayward companion. They were heading for Bethlehem, right reason or none. There was no way *these* kings were going to miss the action. Their journey was well planned, round the back of the P2s, into the middle of the drama, and straight into Bethlehem's manger-square. They walked with style, slowly, well-rehearsed, in time to the music, ready to present their gifts when the singing ended.

The two Kings were doing fine and all was going well, until the dressing-room door burst open and, falling through it, came the *third* king – cloak flapping, present for the baby Jesus tucked jauntily under his arm, cardboard crown at a crooked angle, and LATE! (Why, no one ever figured out, though a P2 teacher was seen in tears later on! Artistic temperament, perhaps?)

Well, this third king may have been guilty of tardiness, of an inability to follow instructions, or of falling out with his teacher, but he was not short of intelligence. Any fool could see that there was no way he could get to Bethlehem by the time the music was finished and meet up with his two companions ready for the next dramatic scene. So he decided he would take a short cut – right through three rows of P1 choristers. Now that might have been OK if the P1s knew he was coming, or if a teacher had got there soon enough to make a suitable gap, or if the recalcitrant king hadn't decided to run at full tilt. But the kids weren't ready for this intrusion, and the teacher wasn't alive enough to the dangers, and the king didn't fancy walking.

So he ran, tripped over a stray P1 leg, fell, skidded along a slippery floor, and arrived at the manger in time to join his more sedate regal companions. But, having arrived, he couldn't stop arriving. He continued to slide, right into the stable, right up to the manger, right into the lap of the suitably surprised Mary. The manger went one way, the precious gift of frankincense went another. A cardboard crown appeared in Joseph's lap, and the baby Jesus, free now of the restrictions of his swaddling bands, rolled gently towards the front row of the somewhat startled Primary 2s.

Teachers ran to the rescue. A clever pianist continued with some incidental music until a semblance of order was restored. The final carol was sung. The star performers took their bow – to the most thunderous applause anyone could ever recall at a school Christmas Nativity Play. And one tear-stained parent was heard to remark that the schoolchildren that year had given her one of the best Christmas presents she'd ever had!

Presents

Auntie Flo brought socks again this Christmas …
well, it's a tradition,
for that's been my present from Auntie Flo
every single year
for as long as I can remember …
hairy ones she'd knitted
from her usual
odd balls of wool
and folded in tissue-paper
and hidden under the cushions of the sofa
for months and months,
well pressed by every bottom that had rested there,
and now mine,
ready to join the dozens of other pairs -
as yet unworn –
and all the right size, though …
How did she know that?

I gave Auntie Flo Freesia Talc again this Christmas ...
well, it's a tradition,
for that's been my present to Auntie Flo
every single year
for as long as I can remember ...
old woman's smelly talc,
bought at the Church
Christmas Fair
and wrapped in gaudy, glossy paper,
(kept in the kitchen cupboard
for months and months,
since we'd bought it half-price last January) ...
and now hers,
ready to join the dozens of other tins of talc,
(I'll bet, unused ...)
and all the right fragrance, though ...
How did I know that?

I got a kiss from Auntie Flo this Christmas,
and I kissed her back ...
well, it's a tradition,
for we've kissed each other
every single year
for as long as I can remember ...
and hugged too,
and smiled a lot,
and giggled,
dressed in silly party hats ...
and we've remembered it for months and months,
long after Christmas is over
for another year,
when January has come and gone ...

and now ours,
ready to join the dozens of other hugs and kisses –
well worn –
and all the right kind of loving, though …
How did we know that?

Christmas Day

Old Testament: Isaiah 9:2-7
Epistle: Titus 2:11-14
Gospel: Luke 2:1-20

6 Why?

'What you doin'?' Nathan asked. Trevor throttled back the big petrol mower when he realised that Nathan was pulling at the leg of his jeans. The mower spluttered, coughed, spluttered again, coughed, and stopped. The unexpected silence was broken only by a whispered but heartfelt 'Damn!' as Trevor anticipated another struggle to get the old machine started.

'What you doin', Trebor?' Nathan asked again. (He never *could* get the name right!) Trevor and Nathan were best mates – or at least they *usually* were, barring Nathan-inspired interruptions. Trevor worked in the grounds of the big house, the De Vries family home. It was a summer job that more than adequately filled the long months during his break from college, and it was the second year Trevor had been employed in the expanded summer gardening squad. The big house had extensive grounds, and, given that the gardens were open to the public from July to September, extra hands were needed to do the routine gardening stuff, like hedge-trimming, weed-clearing and, of course, grass-cutting.

Nathan and Trevor had met the previous summer. Nathan had just turned five back then. He was the grandson of the house's owner and he'd come to stay with his family for a summer beak. *And* he was the most inquisitive child Trevor had ever met. You would have thought that a year-long programme of questions since then – for Trevor expected no less from 'Mister Questioning' – would have made Nathan run out of things to ask about. But six-year-olds obviously ask as many questions as five-year-olds. So, here was Nathan, at it again.

'What you doin', Trebor?' Nathan was still enquiring. 'I'm cutting the grass – or at least I *was* till a moment ago.' 'Why you cuttin' the grass?' 'Because it's long and it needs to be shorter,' Trevor explained, well used to this kind of questioning. 'Why's it long?' Nathan continued. 'Because it grows in the summer.' 'Why's it grow?' 'Well … (Trevor could see several hours of his working day being taken up with this line of questioning …) it's all to do with the rain and the sun, 'cause that's what plants need to grow. And grass is a kind of plant, and when the sun shines and when it rains, the grass grows, and when it's long it doesn't look right, so it needs to be cut, and that's what I'm doing now.'

Trevor hoped his minimal grasp of horticultural theory and the forceful tone of his voice would signal to Nathan that the questioning should end. Nathan was silent for a bit. Trevor felt he'd cracked it – until Mister Questioning started again.

'Do I grow 'cause the sun shines and the rain falls? My Nan says I shouldn't go out in the rain 'cause I'll get wet and catch a chill. So I didn't get wet for ages and ages, but I still growed and growed. Is it 'cause I have a bath and get wet? Is that the same as getting rained on to make me grow, 'cause my Nan says I'm growed a whole lot since last year.'

'No, Nathan, *you* don't grow because of sun and rain – or bathwater, come to that. You grow because you eat well, and your body grows because it's healthy …' Trevor realised that his grasp of anatomy and physiology was as limited as his knowledge of horticulture. Nathan was quiet. He was thinking. Had Trevor's limited knowledge been enough? No such luck …

'Why's my Nan got different colour hair from you?' *'Eh?'* thought Trevor, *'And where on earth did that question come from?'* 'Everyone has different colour hair,' he replied. 'It's what makes us different from each other.' 'My Nan's got different colour hair from what she had last summer,' Nathan continued. 'Oh?' Trevor offered, not knowing what else to say. 'Why?' 'Why what?' 'Why's my Nan got different colour hair? You said it's what makes us different. Why's she changed it?' *'Has* she?' Trevor enquired. Nathan nodded. 'Last year it was silvery, and now it's orange. Why?'

Trevor had lost the will to live. And he'd certainly run out of patience. Too many questions from a small boy. Too much enquiring. Too much of everything …

The situation was rescued by a shout from across the lawn. 'Nathan! Nathan! Lunch time! Come on, quickly now!' It was the lady with the orange hair. Nathan looked at Trevor, disappointment clearly showing in his eyes. 'Why do I have to go for lunch?' 'Because, if you don't eat, you don't grow, and if you don't grow, the grass'll be bigger than you, and then you'll be lost, and I might run over you with the lawn-mower …' But Nathan was gone, hot-footing it home for lunch with his orange-haired Nan, and not turning back even once, just in case the story about the lawn-mower turned out to be true.

That was thirty years ago. Trevor ended up as a head gardener with the National Trust. And he wasn't at *all* surprised when he turned on the TV one night and saw Nathan De Vries on 'Question Time' as the Environmental Spokesman for the Green Party. 'Well,' he mused, 'some things never change.'

Questions

Questions, questions,
Always some more questions,
Struggling with this and that,
And whys and wherefores too …
Questions, questions,
Still a host of questions,
How? and when? and what? and where?
And not forgetting who?

Questions, questions,
Overwhelming questions,
Never knowing when I'll say,

'I've asked enough for now ...'
Questions, questions,
Will I have more questions,
Even when I'm old and shouldn't
Care much anyhow?

Questions, questions?
Yes, I like your questions ...
Come to me, and ask away,
And show you want to learn.
Questions, questions?
Please, ask all your questions ...
And you'll find you come to know
What matters in return.

Questions! Questions!
Never leave your questions
Out of sight from prying eyes
Or from true Wisdom's gaze ...
Questions! Questions!
Find your Way with questions!
Grasp your Truth, fulfil your Life,
With questions all your days.

First after Christmas

Old Testament: 1 Samuel 2:18-20, 26
Epistle: Colossians: 3:12-17
Gospel: Luke 2:41-52

Rodney's carnation

Rodney always wore a carnation in his buttonhole – even when he wasn't going to a wedding - because he wouldn't have felt properly dressed if he didn't. Rodney's carnations weren't always the same colour. You could say his moods were colour-coded ... Pink was the basic colour, the one he would wear the most. He'd choose yellow when he was feeling down and red when he was feeling good. White would be for birthdays and other special occasions.

Recently, Rodney had been wearing yellow carnations a lot. He hadn't worn a red one for ages. Yellow had become his colour of choice.

It was the diagnosis that had taken the stuffing out of him. At least, he suspected the diagnosis wasn't good. The GP hadn't actually *said* so in so many words. 'Better send you for tests,' the doctor had suggested. He didn't really need to say much more. Rodney wasn't stupid. So he'd been wearing a lot of yellow carnations since then.

Sitting in the waiting room at Professor Chandler's Oncology Clinic wasn't much fun. Rodney was on his own. Well, it's not the kind of place you take your best friend for an afternoon out, is it? And no one said much. Well, it's not the kind of place where you engage in casual chit-chat, is it? One by one people were called through to see the Professor until the only ones that were left were Rodney and a family of four on the far side of the room – an adult male wearing a baseball cap (no class, Rodney thought), an adult female sporting a red bandana (even less class ...), and two youngsters, a teenage female (again, the ubiquitous baseball cap ...) and a young boy.

The boy had been staring at Rodney since he'd arrived. The others were buried in various magazines, but the kid passed the time just staring. And for the life of him, Rodney couldn't stop himself staring back - for the little boy was as bald as a coot!

Apparently having had enough of staring, the kid wandered over. None of the rest of the family took any notice. Rodney tried to seem uninterested. The kid was having none of it.

'Why you got a flower stuck to your jacket?' he asked. Rodney couldn't think of a clever answer. The kid didn't seem too bothered. 'I like yellow,' he continued. 'My duvet's yellow. What colour's your duvet?' Again, no answer from Rodney. Again, the kid unconcerned.

'Why you here? You must be here same reason my sister's here. My sister gets medicine from the doctor. It makes her hair fall out. She went dead bald after a bit. So mum and dad decided to shave their hair off as well, so she didn't feel stupid. And I didn't want left out, so I got my hair shaved off too, see?' He ran his hand over his shiny head. 'You gonna have your hair fall out too?' the kid continued, hardly pausing for breath. Rodney self-consciously ran his hand over his full head of hair. 'Maybe,' he whispered, finding his voice for the first time.

'My sister might die, my mum said, and I said "Can I have her iPod, then?" and my mum cried, and she said iPods don't matter because sisters are more important, and I said, "But I don't have an iPod. It isn't fair, eh?" and she said it isn't fair that my sister should be sick – and I didn't have anything to say after that.' He paused for breath. 'Have you got an iPod?' Rodney shook his head. 'Have you got a sister?' 'No,' Rodney replied. 'So what matters to you, then, if you haven't got a sister *or* an iPod?' Rodney didn't have anything to say after that. The kid decided this signalled that the largely one-sided conversation was over. 'Never mind,' the kid concluded, 'you've still got your yellow flower stuck to your jacket.'

'Amanda Brown?' a receptionist called. And two adults and a teenager rose from their seats and moved together into a room beyond – and the kid went too. 'See ya,' he called back over his shoulder.

By the time it was Rodney's turn to see the Professor he'd had a lot of time to think. He only picked up some of what the specialist said – 'Chemotherapy … palliative … time … quality … not to worry …' And afterwards he had even more time to think. But he couldn't stop thinking about 'The Kid', and iPods, and sisters, and carnations, and what matters, and a whole family with bald heads under their baseball caps and bandanas …

And on the way home, Rodney stopped at the flower shop and bought a red carnation.

Gifts

Gifts come in strange ways –
when we least expect them;
when they're hardly needed;
when we're unprepared …

Gifts of hope
in the midst of sadness;
gifts of healing
in the face of brokenness;
gifts of love
in the depths of despair.

Help me to expect the gift of hope
even when I didn't think there'd be one;
make me ready for the gift of healing
even when I didn't know I needed one;
prepare me now for the gift of love
even when I didn't believe love would be enough.

Epiphany

Old Testament: Isaiah 60:1–6
Epistle: Ephesians 3:1–12
Gospel: Matthew 2:1–12

8 A little liturgical twist

Murray Cuthbert hadn't been a Beadle* for long. It had been a long-standing ambition of his to follow in his father's footsteps and be a Beadle in the village church. After all, a Beadle was a *very* important job in the church and carried a fair bit of status locally too. The Church Beadle – the 'minister's man'.

Murray's father had been the Beadle for forty years. When he died, Murray had been away from home, serving in the forces at the end of the war. But even if he had been at home it wasn't likely that he could have taken over as Beadle directly from his father. It would have looked too much like a stitch up – and that would *never* do in the local church. So the Beadle's role had gone to Sandy Innes, the retired postman, and everyone agreed that Sandy had filled the role in exemplary fashion.

When Sandy had to step down, Murray hoped that he would be asked to fill the old man's shoes. It wasn't the kind of job you *applied* for. You had to wait to be approached. So when Murray was approached by the minister to be asked whether he would consider being the Beadle, he was absolutely delighted.

The Sunday Murray Cuthbert was installed as Beadle was the happiest day of his life. It was all he could have wished for. And Murray took the job very seriously indeed. Sunday by Sunday, things were just so. The minister's robes in the vestry would be carefully laid out over the brown leather chair, in front of the warming fire. The hymn-numbers would be placed in the praise board in good time, all spaced accurately to a fraction of an inch. And when it came time to carry in the big Bible, place it in the pulpit, open it to the appropriate

---

* A 'Beadle' is the Scottish Presbyterian equivalent of a Church Warden or a Church Officer.

page, adjust the markers, and then lead in the minister for worship, Murray, with his black gown and upright military bearing, was a Beadle to be proud of.

When the time came for the first baptism in Murray's tenure as Church Beadle, he was well familiar with the style, form and expectations of the church and its minister. Everything was prepared as meticulously as usual. So when Murray led in the baptismal party and took his place discreetly at the side to observe proceedings and be ready to lead the people out again at the appropriate time, he was beaming with pride. Murray loved baptisms, and his first one as the Beadle was a red-letter day indeed.

The minister was in good form. The preamble to the baptism having been intoned with appropriate Presbyterian dignity, the minister stepped forward, took the baby from the Godmother and moved across the chancel to the white marble font - and stopped. The watching Murray knew why. He broke out in a cold sweat. For that's when he realised that he'd forgotten to put any water in the baptismal font.

What was he to do? His precious tenure as Church Beadle could end right at this moment. The minister glanced in his direction. Was that a glower on the stern Presbyterian countenance? Whatever it was, it galvanised Murray into action. With great presence of mind – and appropriate dignity - he moved silently to where the minister stood by the baptismal font, bowed deeply, moved to the side of the chancel and returned a moment later carrying a little jug of water – the water the ladies used to top up the flower-vases before worship began. Once again, he bowed to the minister, turned to the font, calmly filled it with the water from the jug, bowed a third time to the minister, and exited stage-left. The minister, without the slightest appearance of consternation or word of apology, proceeded with the baptism, and, when the service was over, the baptismal party and congregation pronounced themselves satisfied that it had been the most excellent of baptismal services.

Murray was busying himself clearing things up in the church after everyone had gone, when a stranger, a well dressed lady, sought him out. He'd been pondering the un-Presbyterian rollicking he was going to get from the minister and the potential threat this morning's debacle posed for his future as Church Beadle. He didn't need someone else coming to tell him the obvious – that the baptism had been close to being ruined. But the lady didn't look angry. Instead, she held out her hand and, shaking Murray's, introduced herself as the little baby's grandmother. 'This is the first time I've been in my daughter's church,' she said. 'What a lovely service it has been today. And, if I may say, I particularly liked the meaningful liturgical twist of a member of the congregation carrying in the water for the baptism. So special, and so theologically right. Why, I'm going back to my own church next Sunday, and I'm going to say to my own minister, "Why do you not do baptisms the way they do them in my daughter's church, you know, when the water is carried in before the baptism takes place?" We have to do things right, don't you think? So thank you very much indeed.'

Murray was smiling, for he'd begun to work out what his defence was going to be when a stern-faced Presbyterian minister faced him with the accusation of being a poor Beadle and getting the baptism wrong, and he might just mention a little liturgical twist …

Well …

Well, here I am.
standing here, in a good place, watching, waiting.
It's gone well so far.
I'm happy with the progress.
I'm content to stay in the wings, waiting, watching.

But you had more in mind for me than that, didn't you?
So here I am, now centre stage.
Here I stand, not knowing what end is up,
when I'd rather be watching and waiting in the wings.

So forgive me if I appear a bit overwhelmed.
Be patient with me when I don't quite know what's going on.
Understand me when I give the impression
that it's all too much ...

Oh, and this blessing bit,
this voice that I keep hearing when I'm out front,
when I'd rather be in the wings, waiting and watching,
is that for real?

I hope so.
For now I'm here, instead of watching and waiting,
I reckon I'll need all the blessing that's going.

Baptism of our Lord

Old Testament: Isaiah 43:1–7
Epistle: Acts 8:14–17
Gospel: Luke 3:15–22

9 The wedding day

Colin was very fond of Annie Black. She was one of those lovely old ladies he and the rest of the team in the Home just loved looking after. Dignified, uncomplaining, grateful, funny, and much more besides, people like Annie Black were the ones who made nursing worthwhile for Colin. 'If only they were all like that,' the nurses often commented.

Geriatric nursing wasn't easy. Some shifts were long and arduous. Maybe that's why Colin and Annie got on so well. Annie needed Colin and the other nurses. But they all needed Annie too, even if it was just to make sense of the rest of the stuff. Yes indeed, Colin was very fond of Annie Black.

That's probably why he was so affected by the news that Annie's husband had died. It wasn't unexpected, and there was certain to be a sense of relief at his passing. For Annie's husband had had no real quality of life for many years. Willie Black had been suffering from Alzheimer's for a long while, and, in recent times, it had become so bad that he knew nobody, not even his beloved Annie.

He'd been in long-term care for several years and Annie had visited him regularly. But now that she was in long-term geriatric care herself, she was dependent on staff taking her on periodic visits. Not that there was much point, Colin had remarked one day after he'd taken Annie on her visit, for she no longer appeared to be special to Willie Black. He remembered how tearful Annie was on the way back to the Home.

Colin was distressed at the news of Willie's death, but he was even more concerned when he learned that Annie had taken poorly herself, and that, on the doctor's advice, she wasn't going to be able to get to her husband's funeral. That's why he'd responded readily to a request from Annie's sister. 'I was wondering …' she'd said, 'you know

… Willie's funeral is on Thursday at two o'clock … well … if you're working on Thursday … well … you know … I was wondering … could you sit with Annie when the funeral's on? I think she'd like that …' And that's why Colin found himself sitting with Annie on the following Thursday, just before two, in the corner of one of the lounges. To be honest, he didn't know what he was supposed to do. So he did what he thought best … and made them both a cup of tea.

It was just on two o'clock and he was offering Annie a digestive biscuit, when, simply to make conversation, he asked, 'How long were you and Willie married, Annie?' 'Fifty-four years, son,' she replied before taking a mouthful of digestive. And before taking a biscuit of his own, Colin found himself continuing – and to this day he doesn't know why – 'I'll bet you can remember your wedding day as if it was yesterday!' Annie smiled and carefully placed the remains of her digestive in her saucer. 'I can that,' she grinned. 'D'you want to hear about it?' 'I certainly do,' said Colin. And so the story of Annie and Willie's wedding began.

'It was in the minister's hoose, in his front room,' Annie began, 'wi' me and ma man, his brither and ma sister as the witnesses, an' his folks and mine tae mak' sure it was a' in order.' 'Not a church wedding, then?' Colin enquired. 'Naw, son. Big, fancy weddin's were no for the likes o' us. An' then it was back tae ma mither and faither's hoose for steak pie and peas, a flagon o' beer, an' a fiddler in the corner for the entertainment.'

Colin listened with rapt attention. 'Did you have a honeymoon after it was all over?' he asked – at a convenient point when Annie had paused for breath. 'Honeymoon? Naw, son. We didnae dae that in ma day. Nae money for the likes o' that,' she laughed. 'So what did you do after the celebrations?' Colin probed, mirroring Annie's smile. 'Well, you see,' Annie continued, with a twinkle in her eye, 'me an' Willie had a room at ma sister's hoose, so we went up there, just him and me.'

By now, Annie Black was grinning from ear to ear. 'Is that so?'

Colin grinned back 'Well, I don't think I should hear any more, for I have a funny feeling I'll just get embarrassed.' 'Och, away wi' ye, laddie. Fur I'll tell you that bit an' a' ...' Colin was conscious of his cheeks reddening. 'Well, when we got there – tae ma sister's hoose, ye ken - I got the kettle tae mak' me an' Willie a cup-o'-tea. An' when we wis waitin' for the tea, I sat on his knee an' I stroked his hair.' 'Stroked his hair? Is that all?' Colin asked, with a twinkle in his own eye now. 'Weel, laddie, whit mair wis I to be aboot? For I had just turned seventeen, an' I didnae ken onything aboot onything. So I stroked his hair. For Willie wis a fairmer's laddie, and his lang hair wis bleached blond wi' the sun. An' that's why I'd fallen fur him. So I sat on his knee, for ages and ages, an' a stroked his hair, an' efter that we drank oor tea.' 'And then?' an intrigued Colin asked. 'An' then ...' Annie responded, 'an' then ...' She paused for what seemed like an age. Then her wrinkled old face broke into the widest grin Colin had ever seen on Annie Black's face. 'An' then ... we finished oor tea, tidied up, an' went back tae ma mither an' faither's for the rest o' the party!'

Annie sank back in her chair and started to laugh, a deep, croaky, old lady's laugh. She took hold of Colin's hand, and as he moved his hand more comfortably towards hers he caught sight of his wristwatch. It showed 2.30. The funeral service would be over. But through it all, Annie Black, bereaved of her husband, had remembered her wedding day, and had been a teenage bride again, and had been very, very close to a young, blond-haired farmer's boy called Willie Black.

When we were one

When we were newly one, we took the time
To nurture love in joyful, carefree days,
To live one life and share each other's ways ...
When we were good, each moment was sublime.

When we were young at heart, we made the choice
To venture forth and drink the best of wine,
And find that place where heaven and earth combine ...
When we were one, we made the world rejoice.

When we could trust our love, we joined the dance
That leads to family life with children's cries,
And coped with sweet hellos and sad goodbyes ...
When we were right, we offered life the chance.

When we were in our prime, we valued more
Of what was deep and lasting in our years,
And found a different love in joy and tears ...
When we grew old, we had our treasure store.

When we were older yet, in each embrace
We found we'd saved the best of wine till last,
A love so rich it could not be surpassed ...
When we are one, we're ever blessed by grace.

Second after Epiphany

Old Testament: Isaiah 62:1-5
Epistle: 1 Corinthians 12:1-11
Gospel: John 2:1-11

10 The shoes

Malcolm wasn't a bad kid. Like all the rest of the kids in the street he could get up to his fair share of mischief. He would be first to duck into a stairwell with the rest of the lads when the police car was spotted – even though he knew he'd done nothing to be picked up for. Well, he *was* one of the crowd, wasn't he? And running away was easier than explaining things, wasn't it?

The youth club was the making of Malcolm. Run by the church in a redundant portacabin in the playground of the local school, it was the best thing since sliced bread. Evenings were given over to playing pool and chatting up the local talent. But it was the school-holiday afternoons that Malcolm enjoyed the most. The youth club leaders had seen possibilities in Malcolm and had recruited him to be a 'helper', a kind of assistant leader, when it was the turn of the younger kids to use the youth club portacabin. And Malcolm had blossomed. He had quickly grown into the role and showed great potential for the future. He loved it.

Which was just as well … for Malcolm didn't have much going for him at home, and he and his two younger brothers made the best of a difficult upbringing. They were survivors, and being an apprentice youth club leader was just what Malcolm needed.

So it puzzled the club leaders when Malcolm didn't appear for the Thursday afternoon junior youth club pool tournament. He was usually the first there, getting things ready before the other kids arrived. And this day in particular, he was to be the main man – for Malcolm was the organiser and tournament referee. So, with the pool table at the ready, the youngsters prepared to do battle and the youth club leaders getting to grips with things, it was strange, to say the least, that there was no sign of Malcolm.

The event progressed, however – well, it had to, or there would have been a riot – and a winner was duly crowned. When the crowds had departed and the portacabin had been locked up, there was still no sign of Malcolm. So the decision was made by the club staff to call round to his house on the way home, just to see what was amiss. It was Malcolm who opened the door.

'Malcolm?' began the enquiry. 'You OK? Where've you been? We missed you at the club.' Malcolm looked sheepish.

'Sorry, guys. Couldnae come the day.'

'Have you not been well?' the doorstep questioning continued.

'Naw, it's just that … well … see …'

'C'mon, Malcolm. Out with it. What's been the matter with you?'

'Well … see … it's like this …' Malcolm paused, looked down at his stocking feet, and blurted out, 'Ah couldnae come, see … 'cause ma dad's gone oot wi' the shoes …'

There was a long silence while the truth of the confession had its effect. 'What do you mean, your "dad's gone out with the shoes"? What shoes, Malcolm?'

'*The* shoes,' Malcolm retorted, 'the *only* shoes. Me an' ma dad have the same size feet and we've only got wan pair o' decent shoes between us. An' he's got a doctor's appointment up at the surgery the day, so ah hud nae shoes. So, nae shoes, nae goin' oot. Nae goin' oot, nae club. Happy noo, eh?'

'Sorry Malcolm, we didn't know.' But the reply was offered to a closed door, a shoeless and clearly embarrassed Malcolm having already retreated into the safety of his home.

Later that week the youth club leaders had to give a presentation to the church folk with a view to securing the future of the Porta-cabin Youth Club with funding for another year. There were the usual questions. There were the predictable supporters. And there were the familiar murmurs about 'waste of money …' and complaints about 'spoon-feeding kids …', 'other priorities …', 'never come to church …', and the like. It was the same every year, another skirmish to be fought, another lot of convincing to be done.

One of the leaders had heard it all before. This time he'd had enough. He listened carefully to the moans for what seemed an age. Then he took a big, deep breath, stood up before the people and began, 'You wonder why we need to bother about the kids in our community? Let me tell you a story about a young man just round the corner from here who has to share a pair of shoes with his dad ...'

Blessed are the poor

Blessed are the poor,
even when they share a pair of shoes with someone else!

But what's blessed about that,
when one person has nothing
and another has it all –
down to a pair of shoes for yourself?

Blessed are the poor,
when they challenge our attitudes and complacency ...
we who can walk towards the poor
only if we want to,
and walk away again and do nothing,
because we have the shoes.

Blessed are the poor,
only if they know the Kingdom of Heaven
because we are prepared to walk in *their* shoes,
even the ones they share with someone else.

Third after Epiphany

Old Testament: Nehemiah 8:1-3, 9-12
Epistle: 1 Corinthians 12:12-31*a*
Gospel: Luke 4:14-21

11 The basket-maker

Gerry Black had been a basket-maker. But that was in the days before chain-stores, mass production, foreign imports and ubiquitous plastic. So making baskets was a thing of the past for Gerry, a thing of the long-distant, almost forgotten past. 'Gerald Black, Esquire, Bespoke Basket-Maker' had been the sign over his well-stocked shop in Edinburgh's Stevenson Street, the outside festooned with quality wicker baskets of all shapes and sizes and for every purpose under the sun. But that was now a hazy memory, and the shop, like the street itself, had long since been demolished to make way for expanding university accommodation. For the truth of it was that Gerry Black had been down on his luck for many, many years.

It wasn't the reduction in the bespoke basket trade that had been Gerry's downfall, nor the demolition of his shop and all the others that had filled the streets and alleyways of his part of the city. That had been the start of it, right enough. But the drink had done the rest, and it had done plenty of damage to Gerry Black.

Homelessness for Gerry had become a way of life. Homeless men were figures of revulsion, labelled 'dossers' and 'winos', and to be avoided at all costs. Indeed, there were parts of the city which had been left to become the favoured haunts of the city's homeless, most of whom, unable to get a bed in a Salvation Army hostel or a Lodging House Mission, were reduced to sleeping rough – 'doing an outsider' – in the closes, stairs and back yards of the city's undesirable areas.

Timothy hated the dossers. Indeed, he would go out of his way to avoid them, and if, by chance, he was to come across one late at night when he was on his way home from his studies at the university library, he would quickly cross the road for fear of contamination from one of the city's low-life. It was the only thing that had disturbed him about the city which had become his student home.

Everything else was just great. But dossers and winos were a blight on a beautiful city and a horror in his own life.

That's why Timothy would find it hard to explain why he became friends with Gerry Black. It started when Timothy was waiting for a bus and saw a bedraggled old figure emerge from an alleyway next to the bus shelter. He was about to dismiss the pathetic figure as 'another dosser' when he realised that the old man was carrying a bundle of canes under his arm. Timothy watched with growing fascination as the old man divested himself of his mangy coat and laid it carefully on the pavement at the corner of the street. He sat down, and, placing his bundle of canes by his side, carefully pulled out three strands and started to plait them together.

Timothy couldn't quite make out what was going on, but could see clearly enough that something was taking shape in the old man's hands. Whatever it was, before it was completed, it was laid carefully on the pavement while the old man rummaged in the pocket of his coat. Extricating something with obvious glee, he returned to his creation, somehow incorporating his new find into the object of his attention. Then, the work done, he snipped off the ends of the canes with a knife also retrieved from his coat pocket and held the finished object in front of his face to inspect it carefully. He shook it from side to side, and Timothy realised that what the old man had made was nothing other than a wickerwork baby's rattle - the rattle made from his canes; the rattling noise coming from three bottle-tops.

That was the first of many rattles Timothy watched Gerry Black make over the next three years. For Timothy got to know Gerry very well indeed. Arthritis in his fingers meant that Gerry could only do one or two rattles a day, and, even then, they didn't bring in much money. But Gerry was a proud man, and felt that begging was beneath him. Selling rattles was fine; begging and offering nothing in return was not. He wouldn't even take money from Timothy, even though Timothy pressed him often enough. And that's why Timothy accumulated more wickerwork baby's rattles with bottle-tops in them than he'd care to admit.

Gerry Black had no place to lay his head. Timothy would think of the old man 'doin' an outsider' while *he* was tucked up in his warm student flat. He would think of an old basket-maker in his 'glory days, when life wis braw', and think of him sitting on his coat at a street corner, reduced to making rattles for children. He would think of a society that had rejected Gerry Black, and wondered where things had gone wrong.

When Timothy returned to the university for his final year Gerry Black was nowhere to be found. During the first few weeks of term Timothy searched Gerry's usual haunts, but he never saw the old basket-maker again. No one knew what had happened to Gerry Black.

Timothy hasn't kept any of Gerry Black's rattles. He wishes he had, but they probably wouldn't pass the 'health and safety' test for his grandchildren anyway. But, when they're big enough, he'll tell his grandchildren about Gerald Black Esquire, Bespoke Basket-Maker, and make sure *they* know what a city can do to an old master craftsman.

Discarded

Down through the West Port and into the Market,
See old Gerry come shuffling along,
Old shoulders covered with faded grey overcoat,
Wondering why the nights are always so long.

'Tell me, old man, have you eaten this morning?'
'Naw, son, ah huvnae eaten a bite,
Fur ah huvnae nae money nor bed tae lie doon on.
Ye see, that's why ah did an ootsider last night.'

O God, keep you safe, my friend, old Gerry Black.
No one makes rattles for children like you.

Where, where will this great Festive City end up
Now old Gerry Black has gone too?

Your fingers are bent; your canes are all broken;
You're only fit to make rattles now.
And the people walk by and pretend they don't see you;
They leave you there to get by on your own anyhow.

'There once wis a time ah made baskets fur gentry.
Aye, son, but things are no whit they were.
The canes that they gie me are just fit fur firewood –
Ach, my son, d'ye really think that it's fair?'

O God, keep you safe, my friend, old Gerry Black.
No one makes rattles for children like you.
Where, where will this great Festive City end up
Now old Gerry Black has gone too?

Down through the West Port and into the Market,
All through the Cowgate and up to the Tron,
No one comes shufflin' with faded grey overcoat,
No one makes rattles here now that old Gerry has gone.

And who will remember the worker who's worthless,
Discarded by gentry, ignored by the crowd,
Broken and twisted like canes that are useless?
'Just fit fur firewood' – for him, it's his only reward.

O God, keep you safe, my friend, old Gerry Black.
No one makes rattles for children like you.
Where, where will this great Festive City end up
Now old Gerry Black has gone too?

And now as I sit at my chic pavement table,
Amidst trendy wine bars, a city in song,

Surrounded by people, all bent to their pleasure,
I still see an old basket-maker come shuffling along.

But now he is proud, with the bearing of affluence,
A prosperous gentleman, so they all say.
It's Gerald Black Esquire, Bespoke Basket-Maker –
'Ach son, sit doon, an' ah'll mak' ye a rattle the day ...'

O God, keep you safe, my friend, old Gerry Black.
No one makes rattles for children like you.
Where, where will this great Festive City end up
Now old Gerry Black has gone too?

Fourth after Epiphany

Old Testament: Jeremiah 1:4-10
Epistle: 1 Corinthians 13:1-13
Gospel: Luke 4:22-30

12 Chosen

Jack loved football. His granny's second cousin had played for Tottenham Hotspur in the 1930s, and though Jack never even knew where Tottenham was, it sounded very romantic and special. One of the first things he could remember was kicking a ball with his dad in the back yard. When he grew older, his bedroom walls were covered with pictures of his heroes, newspaper cuttings of his favourite team, and huge posters from the World Cup and European Championships.

But Jack was rubbish at football. Try as he would, he had no coordination when it came to kicking a ball. You want to know how to kick a ball sideways when you want it to go straight? Ask Jack. You want to know what a fresh-air shot is? Ask Jack. You want to know what it feels like to be told by your dad that 'you kick a ball like a girl'? Ask Jack.

The worst thing of all was waiting to be chosen when teams were being picked for a kick-about in the school playground. The two best players always picked the teams, of course, and the kids would stand by the school wall patiently waiting their turn to be selected. Jack would always be there. (Would be never learn?) One by one – the best ones first, then the biggest and strongest, then the rest at random – the teams would be picked, until only Jack was left. And the ultimate embarrassment was that, even as the last one, he wouldn't be selected at all, and the kids would just turn away ready to get on with their game. Jack would watch from the sidelines pretending it didn't matter – but it always did. It wasn't that Jack didn't have any friends. It was just that he was rubbish at football, and who wants a rubbish football player on your team?

Jack's great hero was Janek Danowski. 'Big Dan', as Danowski was known by his adoring fans, had settled in the town after the war. He'd been a Polish schoolboy international and, now in his mid-twenties, had been snapped up by the city's premier club. He was *the* star player and had been the main reason why the club had won the league championship for the first time in thirty years. Big Dan scored goals for fun and, a thoroughly nice guy, was the role model any parent would have been pleased for their kids to follow.

Imagine the excitement, therefore, when word went round that Janek Danowski was to come to visit Jack's school to show the pupils the League Trophy and to run a training session for the school team. 'Big Dan, coming *here*, to *my* school … ?' Jack wondered. But the rumours were confirmed when, at the school assembly on the Monday morning, the head teacher announced that the great Janek Danowski was to come to the school right enough – and the very next day!

Jack couldn't contain his excitement. He never slept a wink on the Monday night and was up with the lark on the Tuesday morning. He was not to be disappointed. When the whole school gathered in the gym hall and Janek Danowski walked in carrying the huge League Trophy, the cheer was the loudest thing Jack had ever heard. Sitting cross-legged in the very front row with Big Dan towering above him he almost wet himself as he clapped and cheered with all the rest. His greatest ever hero … right here in front of him … It was almost too much to believe.

Janek Danowski stood holding the cup aloft, just as he'd done at the end of their league-winning season. Jack hoped he would look at him, so his great hero could, just for a moment, recognise he was there. But the problem with being little and being right in the front row is that people look over the top of you and catch the eyes of the big kids at the back. So Jack just cheered and clapped and watched. That would have to be enough.

Big Dan held his arms above his head one final time while the cheering subsided, the big cup in one hand and the other hand in a clenched-fist salute. And that's when it happened … In all the excitement Janek Danowski didn't realise that he was carrying the cup at a dangerously tilted angle. Indeed, no one realised it until the cup tipped over too far and the big silver top slipped off. The head teacher noticed it, but too late. Almost in slow motion, the top detached itself from the cup and landed – right in Jack's lap! He didn't *try* to catch it. He'd just dropped his hands on to his lap for a bit because they were sore with clapping and he needed to give them a rest. And before he realised what was happening, the top of the League Trophy was nestling safely in his hands.

'Good caught!' shouted a booming voice as Big Dan bent down to retrieve the fallen top of the cup. At least everyone *thought* he was going to pick up the lid but, instead, a big arm scooped up a little boy in the front row with a silver cup's lid in his hands. Then, placing the cup carefully on the floor, Big Dan held Jack aloft where a moment earlier he had brandished the League Trophy. He took the cup's lid and placed it decorously on Jack's head. All the kids laughed, and so did Jack. 'A new trophy for now, you think?' boomed Big Dan. 'This man have good catch. Maybe he be our goalkeeper one day, you think?' All the school cheered – the second loudest cheer Jack had ever heard.

Later that day Jack stood against the playground wall as usual and watched the other kids play football, coached by the great Janek Danowski. But Jack didn't mind. Because he'd always remember the day *he'd* been chosen by Big Dan, even though he never really understood why. And maybe one day, who knows, the little man with the good catch might go on to even greater things.

The call

I seek the call, that I might swift obey;
await the call, that I might go your way.
I need the call, that I might be fulfilled;
absorb the call, that I might do your will.

I know the call, and wonder, 'Is it me?'
question the call, and future clear to see.
I doubt the call, and, chosen, wonder 'Why?'
Defer the call, and hold back my reply.

I hear the call, but know not what it says;
accept the call, yet fall in disarray.
I grasp the call, but know not what to do;
affirm the call, yet doubt if it is true.

I trust the call, and go where I am bid;
agree the call, whose secrets still are hid.
I heed the call, and for more guidance pray;
adjudge the call, saying 'Yes, this is your way.'

Fifth after Epiphany

Old Testament: Isaiah 6:1-13
Epistle: 1 Corinthians 15:1-11
Gospel: Luke 5:1-11

13 The climb

It had been a long climb – well, long enough for a man who was unfit and with dreadfully sore feet. It had *sounded* like a good idea when it had come up three months before in the pub with the lads. 'Should do something …', 'Charity stuff …', 'Need to get ourselves sorted …', 'Sponsored kind of thing …', and it went on from there. The result had been a decision to organise a sponsored climb up Ben Nevis – 'Make a weekend of it …', 'It'll be worth it …', 'The bigger the better …', 'Size *is* everything …'. It all sounded like such a good, laudable, generous idea - or at least it *had* …

Half way up – or, if he was honest, about a *quarter* of the way up – Vic wasn't at all sure it had been anything remotely approaching a good idea. Simply put, Vic was unfit, overweight and not much into climbing mountains. He'd promised himself he'd do some training but time had caught up with him somewhat. All he'd managed to do was to stop taking the car to the paper shop in the morning – even though that was only at the top of his road. He'd bought the proper climbing boots on eBay, but he'd never had them on his feet till the morning of the climb! And boy, was that something he regretted …

He'd got his sponsorship sorted out without any problem. The folk in the office had been great – even though he'd had to run the gauntlet of 'You! Ben Nevis? No chance!'; 'I'd like to give you a million quid if you made it, but £50 quid's yours if you do.'; or simply, 'That's the funniest idea I've ever heard …' Maybe that's why people had been so generous. Vic was happy to be the butt of humour for a good cause. It was the least he could do.

'The least he could do …' would have been to fork out the sponsorship money himself and stay in the pub waiting for the others to come back. But bravado, commitment, stupidity and the potential loss of face meant … well … he had to do the climb!

They'd given themselves four hours to get to the top – generous, they all said. But they hadn't figured on Vic, and Vic hadn't figured that being out of condition would play such a major part in this flaming effort. The lads had been understanding and one or other of them had held back to keep Vic company. But their understanding had worn thin, and for the past hour or so Vic had been on his own. It wasn't that the climbing was difficult, it was just that it was so *long*, and his feet were so *sore*, and his spirits were so *low*.

The estimated four hours had come and gone. By Vic's calculation he was still a long way from the summit. What was he to do? Give up? Tell the folk back home he'd made it and claim the sponsor money anyway? Carry on, no matter how long it would take, and incur the wrath of the other lads because he had taken ages? He sat down at the side of the path and put his head in his hands. It was just all too hard …

He was conscious of a young woman standing by his side. She was fit, smiling and cheery. 'Hard work, eh?' 'Aye, too hard,' Vic replied, not greatly appreciating the interruption. 'Never mind, you're nearly there, just about ten minutes or so, round the next corner and over the ridge. I've been up and down the Ben more times than I've had hot breakfasts. It looks like it's your first time.' 'And the bloody last!' Vic grunted. 'Ok, then. I'll be your guide for these last few metres. C'mon, you can do it.' And with that, Vic's new-found companion offered him her hand and Vic was helped gently to his feet.

Over the next ten minutes or so Vic's tiredness began to fall away and, almost with a spring in his step, he made the final few metres to the summit. When he saw the lads his spirits soared. When they saw him there was spontaneous applause and much back-slapping all round. Vic was on top of the world – or at least on top of the UK – and as he soaked in the atmosphere, he confessed to his mates that he had never felt better.

Eventually it was time to face the descent. Vic was reluctant, not because of his tiredness or apprehension about the return journey …

it was just that he wanted to savour the moment a bit longer, to hold on to the feeling of achievement for as long as possible.

He was sitting on a rock nursing his reluctance to go down when he became conscious, for the second time that day, of a young woman by his side. 'It's hard to leave once you've made it, isn't it?' his erstwhile climbing companion remarked. 'But we'll have to get going soon. The weather will close in shortly. Better to get on while it's fine. C'mon, I'll chum you on the way down. But I'll tell you this. You will never, ever forget today. You'll feed on this first-time achievement when you're back down there. Never lose this success, no matter what happens. This is one to tell your grandchildren about. C'mon climber-man, let's go.'

There was much hilarity and sharing of congratulations in the pub that night. But the lads noticed that Vic had spent most of the evening in the company of a young woman none of them could remember ever having seen before.

The summit

Lord, it is good that I am here
on top of the mountain of my achievement,
the pinnacle of my hopes,
the summit of my expectations.

Lord, it is good that you are here,
on top of the mountain of your revelation,
the pinnacle of your truth,
the summit of your love for me.

Lord, it is good that we are here ...
so let me build a shelter now,
to hold this moment of success,
and shelter you and me together.

Lord, it is good that we stay here,
protected from what is yet to come,
down there in the valley,
back home, at the start of another climb.

Transfiguration

Old Testament: Exodus 34:29–35
Epistle: 2 Corinthians 3:12–4:2
Gospel: Luke 9:28–43

14 Beauty from the ashes

Grown men wept as they stood and watched the church go up in flames. And the weeping was not to be confined to the evening of the fire, for when the building was safe enough for a detailed inspection three days later, many tears were shed as folk walked through the ashes of their precious church.

The whole roof had gone, leaving only the charred roof beams. The choir-stalls had been destroyed, and the stained-glass window in the chancel was badly damaged, with much of the lead-work melted by the heat and the coloured glass scattered in broken pieces among the rubble. A fallen roof-tile was embedded in the wooden baptismal font, and many of the pews were beyond rescuing.

It would take three years before the church was restored to its former glory. But that was very far from people's minds. In those initial, devastating days, many tears were shed and many expressions of anger and devastation shared. Hopelessness was the all-pervading theme.

Not so for David Innes. Of course he'd shed tears at the devastation and had expressed anger with the best of them. He was only human after all. The destruction of his church was the worst thing he could remember happening to him. But as David walked through the ashes of his beautiful church, he saw potential where others saw ruins, possibilities while others were stuck at the destruction. Simply put, he saw hope when many did not.

That's why, when the building was being cleared prior to the beginning of the restoration programme, David Innes liberated some of the charred roof timbers. No one knew why, and, if they'd taken any notice, no one would have bothered much anyway. They'd just have thought he was helping with the clear-up like the others. But David was a wood-turner and saw something of beauty and hopefulness in the ashes.

It would take three long, arduous years before the church was restored to its former glory. There were disappointments along the way, much tiredness to be coped with and uncertainties to be faced. But they made it, and a ruined church was eventually restored.

On the night of the reopening of the church and its rededication for worship, David Innes was there with the others, rejoicing in the restoration of his own church. But, as well as his pleasure, David had brought some gifts to the celebration - several simple wooden bowls, turned from the very charred timbers he'd taken away three years before. The bowls were expertly made and beautiful in their form and shape. But they weren't perfect, for they still carried in their tender curves the scorch marks the fire had left on the timbers. There had been no pretence in David's wood-turning. The marks of the fire and the memory of the disaster were always going to be there.

Grown men wept as they gazed in wonder at the beauty and vibrancy of their restored church. But tears of pleasure were also shed as several of them looked in wonder and hopefulness at their gift of a simple, wooden bowl, a symbol of beauty from the ashes they held in their hands.

David Innes didn't want any thanks. He'd done what he had to do. Maybe anyone with the right skills could have turned wooden bowls from fallen roof beams. But David had offered more than just his wooden bowls. For each of his creations was an enduring symbol of the triumph of hope over despair. Beauty from the ashes – now, that has to be worthy of our thanks and praise.

To hold my love for you

'I saw it burn,' God said, on that December night,
'my house, wherein my people dwell.
I saw them gaze, their eyes with horror filled,
and when they wept, I wept with them.

I saw it burn,' God said,
as he looked down one dark December night.

'I saw them walk,' God said, on that December morn,
and raise their eyes to see
the morning sky above the open roof;
and with them wondered what could rise from charred remains.
I saw them walk,' God said,
as he looked down one grey December morn.

'I saw them choose,' God said, as winter days ran on,
'to raise my house again from such remains as these.
I saw them hope and dream, and wonder how and when
all would be for me as once it was.
I saw them choose,' God said,
as he looked on in hopeful winter days.

'I saw them work,' God said, as weeks and months went by,
'when dreams were dimmed and hope was hard to hold.
I willed them on with all I had to give
of love and faith in people such as these.
I saw them work,' God said,
as he looked on in struggling days of toil.

'I saw him love,' God said, in quiet trust,
'when charred remains were turned and shaped
and moulded into beauteous things.
I saw him hold in craftsman's hands the hopes of all
that love would rise again.
I saw him love,' God said,
as he looked on when trust was at the heart of all.

'I saw them come,' God said, on that December eve,
'and offer praise and thanks;

and I rejoiced with them that they were home again.
I saw them smile and weep with joy, at home, in love with me.
I saw them come,' God said,
as he looked on - on that now blessed December eve.

'I saw him hold,' God said, as precious gifts were shared,
'the precious bowl that held the hope and trust in me –
that from the tears and charred remains
could come new shouts of joy and times of beauty still.
And then I knew that we could take
what others count as hopeless trash
and form a home where beauty shines
and people smile, and gifts are shared,
and simple wooden bowls can hold what matters still,
and overflow with hope.

I saw them hold *me* then,' God said,
as he looked on, on that reopening night,
'for then they knew that I had come again,
and love had triumphed over all –
as on that dark December night so long ago
I always knew it would.'

Ash Wednesday

Old Testament: Joel 2:1-3,12-17 *or* Isaiah 58:1-12
Epistle: 2 Corinthians 5:20b-6:10
Gospel: Matthew 6:1-6, 16-21

15 The theft

The biggest theft from the church youth club was also, paradoxically, one of the church's biggest successes. Some of the lads in the parish ran a youth club in the church hall once a week. It wasn't a spectacular success, but it did a good job for some kids who were at risk. The youth club didn't have much by way of funds. That's why there was much celebration when they managed to buy, by means of a small grant from the Council, a six-foot-six, table-top snooker table. It became the pride and joy of the club and a real attraction for the kids who came along. There was talk of a club tournament. Things were looking up.

The youth club had the snooker table for two weeks before it was stolen. Melvin, one of the club leaders, happened to come into the church one lunchtime to be met by the caretaker standing beside an open cupboard. The padlock had been broken off. The snooker table, cues and balls were gone. Nothing else had been taken, only the club's pride and joy. It had been a targeted raid. The snooker table was no more. 'They must have sneaked in when I was cleaning the toilets,' the custodian lamented. 'Did anyone see them?' Melvin enquired. 'No, 'cause no one ever does.'

So it was with a heavy heart that Melvin reported the theft at the local police station. The desk-sergeant was sympathetic but sceptical. 'Broad daylight, you say, and no one saw the perpetrators?' 'No, 'cause no one ever does,' Melvin churned out. So the policeman took the particulars of the stolen snooker table. 'Colour?' he asked. 'Green,' Melvin replied, stating the obvious. 'Size?' 'Six-foot-six by three-foot-three.' 'And no one saw it being taken out of the church?' 'No, 'cause no one ever does,' Melvin repeated the mantra. 'Balls?' the desk-sergeant continued. And deciding it was more a question than a statement Melvin responded, 'Fifteen reds, one yellow, one green …' and rhymed off all the balls, the details of which were appropriately recorded.

The reporting of the theft was completed. 'I'll pass this on to the CID,' Melvin was assured, 'and they'll see what they can do. Mind you, I don't think you'll have much of a chance. You'd think someone would see people in broad daylight carrying a six-foot-six snooker table, but, then …' 'No one ever does', they repeated in chorus.

Melvin left the police station and walked up to the shopping centre. On the way there he met a couple of the lads from the youth club and recounted to them the sorry tale of the stolen snooker table. They were visibly devastated. Gone was the club's prize possession. Gone was the prospect of a club tournament. They were not best pleased. Clearly they felt personally slighted.

Melvin left them and continued his journey to the shops, aware of the fact that, the jungle-drums being what they were, news of the theft from the church would be round the parish in a jiffy. So he wasn't at all surprised when he was accosted by another young lad from the club with the news, 'Did ye hear they nicked the snooker table frae oor church?' Melvin indicated politely to the communicator of this news that he was indeed aware of the tragedy of the theft, and that he didn't reckon there was much chance of getting the table back because nobody had seen the break-in. 'Aye, 'cause naebody ever does, eh?' the lad replied. 'Mind you, I was wonderin' why Toby's brither was asking me half an hour ago if I knew where he could lay his hands on some snooker chalk, eh? An' ah've niver seen ony snooker table in *his* hoose.' Melvin's ears pricked up. 'Toby's brother? Big Toby who comes to the club with you. I didn't know he had a brother.' 'Aye, Yozzer. He's been inside doin' six months for housebreakin', eh.' Melvin's mind was racing. 'Where's he live?' 'Number three, first floor, roon the corner, wi' his burd.' And with that the breathless one-man-news-channel was off.

Melvin pondered his options. Pretty soon he was back at the sceptical desk-sergeant's counter at the local nick. 'Another theft, sir?' the clearly bored officer-of-the-law enquired as Melvin walked in. 'No, sergeant, but some information your CID boys might be interested in. If they were to call, perchance, at the first-floor flat at number three The Crescent, at the home of one Moira Gallagher, they might just find there a young man by the name of Yozzer, or Andrew Robertson, and, if they're quick, they might just catch him before he racks the balls for the second frame of his own personal *Pot Black* on our youth club's snooker table.' 'How d'you know that?' the sergeant enquired, lifting his eyes from his notebook. 'Don't ask,' Melvin suggested. 'But might I encourage your colleagues to act on this information PDQ before Yozzer gets bored with snooker and the table ends up in someone else's hands?'

The youth club got their table back. Yozzer Robertson got three months for the theft. He never grassed up his accomplices, confessing that he'd done the job by himself and carried off his ill-gotten gains on his own – a six-foot-six snooker table, two cues, a racking triangle, one rest, and twenty-one balls … Maybe he made it look so normal that no one thought it was suspicious, or moved so quickly that no one even saw him. After all, no one ever does – eh?

Temptation

'Yield not to temptation!'
That's easy to say!
Much harder to practise
When you're led astray
By many temptations –
Some worse than the rest!
'Yield not to temptation!'
Help, I'm failing the test!

'Yield not to temptation!'
Please God, hear my cry –
I'm useless, no matter
How hard I might try …
You know there is nothing
(Here's a quote from the shelf)
I cannot resist
Except temptation itself.

'Yield not to temptation!'
I'm at my wits' end!
So, choose from your mercy
Some blessing to send
This poor, hapless sinner!
Please help me again!
'Yield not to temptation!'
Quick! I need you! Amen!

First in Lent

Old Testament: Deuteronomy 26:1–11
Epistle: Romans 10:9–13
Gospel: Luke 4:1–13

16 Bessie's plan

Bessie was eighty-seven years old. Everyone knew that, because Bessie took great delight in telling anyone who would listen just how old she was. But nobody minded. She was eighty-seven and proud of it, so that was that. Norrie, on the other hand, was sixty-nine. Everyone knew that too, for most of the local folk had been at Norrie's retirement-cum-sixty-fifth-birthday-party down at the local four years past January. In truth, it was Norrie's two sons' 'do' for their dad and Norrie just turned up as the honoured guest. He nearly drank the pub dry that night – well, it's not every day you retire and turn sixty-five, is it?

Things had gone badly for Norrie since then. His wife of forty years had died within a year of his retirement and Norrie had hit the bottle hard. But it was the cancer that did for him. Years of heavy smoking had taken their toll. Lung cancer had been the result, and Norrie had gone rapidly from a fifteen stone 'fine figure of a man' to a nine stone, emaciated, pathetic old guy.

Not that many people knew that in detail, for Norrie didn't venture out much now. But Bessie knew, for she was the only one who visited Norrie much at all. She was, truth be known, the only one Norrie could be bothered with. Bessie would regularly be seen scurrying from her stair to Norrie's next down but one, carrying a pot of soup, or a steak pie, or the makings of mince and potatoes – 'just taking a wee somethin' to old Norrie to keep his strength up...' – and 'old Norrie' just short of seventy and nearly twenty years her junior!

But it was the knowledge of Norrie's impending 'Big-Seven-O' that made Bessie hatch her plan.

Apart from her pride in her age and concern for Norrie's welfare, Bessie had two passions in life – her church and her bookie's. You daren't ask her which was the more important because she'd never tell you – for fear of offending the people in her alternative congregation.

'Mornin', auld yin,' a cheery counter-clerk offered to Bessie one morning when she came in to put on her daily 'line'. Bessie never bet more than £2 in any one day – big bucks, eh? She knew her limit. 'A pound each way on "Smuggler's Boy" in the 2.30 at Newmarket,' Bessie retorted, 'and enough of your cheek, by the way. Get yourself sorted and tell me what's lyin' for me from yesterday, son.' The clerk did a quick calculation. 'Seven pounds and thirty seven pence,' he chirped. 'A good day, auld … sorry, Bessie.'

Bessie smiled, turned to leave, and was about to pocket her winnings when she stopped. For a moment she was deep in thought. After a bit, she slipped over and had a hurried whispered conversation with the man by the window, an old friend. He nodded and smiled. Bessie returned to the counter. 'Another line?' the clerk enquired, only to be beckoned with a crooked finger. Another close-quarter conversation ensued, followed by a handshake and another big smile. Bessie had many such conversations over the next two weeks. On the Sunday, she similarly accosted several people in her other congregation. There were more nods, a few handshakes, and many smiles. The vicar put his arm round Bessie's shoulder, and after she'd chided him for his familiarity he smiled too.

Norrie's doorbell rang four times on the day of his seventieth birthday. First, it was the postman, refusing to put all the cards for one 'Norman Johnstone' through the letter-box when he could hand over 'the whole bloody bag'. The whole bag contained more birthday cards than Norrie could ever have imagined, from so many folk he knew and lots he'd never even heard of before.

The second time the doorbell rang it was Bessie carrying a small suitcase. Despite Norrie's protests – who would argue with such a woman? – she soon had her bemused neighbour washed, shaved, and dressed in the suit, shirt and tie she'd brought with her.

The third time, the bell announced the arrival of Norrie's family

– two sons, a daughter-in-law, three strapping grandsons, and Norrie's sister from down south whom he hadn't seen since his wife's funeral. Norrie cried and laughed, and ran out of things to say.

So when the doorbell rang for the final time that day and Norrie was ushered into the waiting taxi to take him the short distance to the local pub, Norrie was beyond words. The local was filled to overflowing. There were streamers and balloons, and a big, colourful banner above the bar announcing that someone was seventy years old.

Norrie will tell you he doesn't remember much of that night – and it wasn't the drink either. But he does remember at one point dancing with Bessie, and, as she gently guided him round the pub floor, whispering 'You're still light on yet feet, auld yin,' and Bessie responding with 'An' yer no' too bad for an auld man yersel', Norrie Johnstone,' while she sported the biggest grin Norrie had ever seen.

My soul

Feed my weakened body; hear my cry;
Satisfy me now; don't let me die;
Quench my thirst; restore me; make me whole.
When I'm full, I'll know you've fed my soul.

Heal my damaged mind; don't mute my shout;
Try to understand what I'm about;
Promise me you'll stay and see me whole.
When my mind's my own, you've healed my soul.

Find my true uniqueness; hear my plea;
Don't define my life by what you see;
See beyond a context less than whole.
When you value me, you know my soul.

Body, mind and circumstance need healed,
Fed, restored, rebuilt when love's revealed!
Satisfied, renewed ... Look! I am whole!
Body, mind and spirit – and my soul.

Second in Lent

Old Testament: Genesis 15:1–18
Epistle: Philippians 3:17–4:1
Gospel: Luke 13:31–35

17 The rowan tree

It was never going to be an arduous walk for Wilma. She was an experienced 'Munro Bagger', having climbed most of the Scottish mountains over 3000 feet. So a three-hour walk around the north-west end of the island was no more than an afternoon stroll. And, indeed, that's just what it was, spending a beautiful afternoon walking in the Scottish countryside she'd always enjoyed.

She'd parked the car in the small gravel-covered car park at the end of the single-track road. The map told her the route was clearly marked, taking her out towards the headland, turning south to hit the shore, following the contours of the land to the foot of the cliffs, heading up through the gulley, and from there, over a short stretch of moorland, towards the road and down to the car park.

Wilma was in good spirits, and the views along the track, espe-cially when she reached the headland, were spectacular. She made good time and made sure she stopped often enough to appreciate the views, take some photographs, and think about things that mattered.

It had been hard work clambering up the gulley. The path was dis-tinct enough, but it was steep and rocky in places, and it was harder than she expected. The guidebook had indicated it was the most dif-ficult part of the walk. And so it turned out.

She first noticed the rowan tree when she was almost at the top of the gulley. She saw its green outline with smudges of red berries rise above the horizon of bracken and heather as the steepness of the gulley began to even out. At first it looked like no more than a bush. But as the ground lost its steepness, the rowan tree emerged for what it was – a great, full-grown mountain ash, at the height of its beauty, laden with bunches of bright red berries, and standing proud against the vivid blue of the cloudless sky; a single tree, alone in the expanse of moorland; a bright jewel in the spreading greens and browns of the surrounding countryside.

It wasn't until she was a good deal closer to the lone rowan tree that Wilma saw the ruins of the houses. The tree stood at the corner of what were quite clearly the fallen walls of a homestead. Part of the chimney breast still stood. The ruin had two distinct rooms, with a smaller, single-room outline a few yards to the side. Scattered around, within an area of a few hundred yards or so, were the ruins of a dozen or more buildings. A few were bigger than the others. A couple were better preserved. Some had almost disappeared, with their fallen walls barely visible as the shifting peat and growing bracken claimed them for their own. Around some there were signs of an enclosing wall, the boundary of a field or garden. And, in the middle of it all, like a lone sentinel, the magnificent rowan tree.

Wilma consulted her map. 'Ruin', it said. And that's what she was standing in the middle of for sure. But ruin of what? A village, clearly; a community of people who had once scratched a living from the sea and land; families who had reared their children on the fruit of the soil, in the vastness of the moor, part of the beauty of the good earth. And, amidst it all, someone, at some time, had planted a rowan tree.

Wilma sat on the fallen wall beside the rowan tree and had a think. She remembered the legend that if you planted a rowan tree it would fend off evil spirits and keep your house safe. But what good had this rowan tree done to fend off the evils of economic decline, the ravages of disease, the unfairness of landowners, the rigours of a Scottish winter, and much more besides, any one of which could have been the cause of the clearance of what would once have been a thriving, close-knit, God-fearing community? So, perhaps the rowan tree wasn't the stuff of legend at all.

But what if it could speak? If it could share what it held in the memory banks of its growing years? What if it could tell of the things it had seen and heard, witnessed and looked over, through the passing generations? And as she sat on a ruined wall and looked out over the village, Wilma was sure she could hear the rowan tree whisper of its memories. And, as it did, it told of children playing barefoot in the heather; of rough-coated cattle roaming nearby; of men hauling baskets of fish up the gulley from the shore; of women bashing clothes on the big stone by the burn at washing time; of drams being shared and successes toasted; of women keening and grown men weeping as they buried their own. And a rowan tree told a passer-by of life and laughter, of tears and toil, of comfort and community.

Wilma found it hard to pull herself away from the unnamed, uncared for village at the top of the gulley above the sea. But before she eventually went on her way to complete her walk she touched the sentinel rowan tree and offered her thanks – for all the memories it had whispered to her and all the life, and all the beauty, and all the clarity she'd found that day.

And when she got home, she went to her local garden centre, and bought a tiny rowan tree, which even now, at the corner of her garden, has become a watcher over her home, a sentinel for generations yet to come, and a collector of many, many memories.

A Rowan Tree

In open moorland, there you stand,
Alone, it seems, amidst a land
So bleak and barren, wild and bare,
That never life would venture there.

And yet, you do not stand alone;
For all around, in scattered stone
Of fallen walls and chimney breasts,
Are signs of homes which welcomed guests,

As loving families, with accord,
Shared tears and laughter, bed and board;

Where children played, and cattle roamed
Around the school, and church and home.

Now, rowan tree, alone you stay
To guard these ruins, night and day,
And tell your tales in whispered breath
Of living stones, and not of death ...

For what was good in what was here
No hour or day or month or year
Can e'er erode from memory's cache –
You tell of this, fair mountain ash.

So in the stillness of this day,
I listen as I pass this way,
And hear the rowan speak to me
Of all that was and yet shall be.

Third in Lent

Old Testament: Isaiah 55:1-9
Epistle: 1 Corinthians 10:1-13
Gospel: Luke 13:1-9

18 Elvis leaves the building ...

Elvis was a loveable rogue. Actually, he was often more rogue than loveable, though, thankfully, the changeable 'loveable' part never disappeared completely. Martin Miller knew that. As one of the guidance teachers in the local High School he knew Elvis well and had kept in touch with him and some of the other kids who'd left school the previous year.

'Loveable' for Elvis was variable. The 'rogue' part, however, appeared to be on the increase – or so Martin kept hearing – as Elvis and trouble seemed to be more and more inseparable.

Oh, and before we move on ... the 'Elvis' tag? In actual fact this loveable rogue had been christened the remarkable Andrew Wallace Burns Lenin Presley! (Don't ask why! Try working it out ...) So 'Presley' = 'Elvis'. Simple, eh?

Martin was on his way home from school one Friday afternoon when he was accosted by Terry Cranston, another of the kids Martin knew well from his school days. 'Yo, Mr Miller! Clocking off early, eh? What a skive! An' long summer holidays too, eh?' 'How are you, Terry?' Martin enquired, not bothering to challenge Terry's assumption of an early Friday finish and a teacher's easy life. 'Not bad, not too bad. Better than Elvis, by the way, that's for sure.' Martin was puzzled. 'Elvis?' he queried. 'What's happened to Elvis?' 'Have ye no' heard? He's been lifted ... last week ... local Polis ... caught him an' his brother wi' a van-load o' fags ... roon the back o' the supermarket ... banged up ... waiting for a trial ... in Shortlane ... dozy idiot ... fancy getting' caught ... Anyway, I cannae hang aboot. Huv a good weekend, eh?' And, with that, Terry was off, clearly delighted he'd been the one to impart a juicy piece of news his ex-teacher didn't have already.

The following Monday evening found Martin at Shortlane

Remand Centre waiting somewhat impatiently for Elvis to be brought into the visitors' area. It had been a long wait and Martin was tired and keen to get home. He was not prepared for the sight he saw next.

The door at the far end of the room swung open and in walked a prison warder with a bedraggled Elvis by his side. Was this the Elvis Martin had known in the fullness of a roguish life? For his blond hair had been shorn. He shuffled rather than walked. He wore a faded denim bomber-jacket that was clearly two sizes too big, with cuffs rolled up but with the sleeves still touching his knuckles. And there was no grin or sparkle in his eyes.

He sat down as instructed, across a table from Martin. 'Five minutes,' muttered the warder.

It was the longest five minutes of Martin's Miller's life. Not much was said. Elvis cried. Martin did too. Maybe that was enough. And by the time Elvis was shuffled out of the visitors' room to face his uncertain future, Martin had made a decision – the loveable bit of this loveable rogue would get his full attention and commitment from now on. And the rogue part? Well, that would just have to wait its turn.

For, strangely enough, with cropped hair, and shuffling gait, and way-too-big denim top, the loveable side of Elvis had gone way up off the scale.

Confession

God,
I've messed up again.
See me,
this loveable rogue you created?
Why did you make me like this,
where the loveable always struggles with the rogue bit,
and I fail?

God,
I've been found out again.
See me,
this shuffling failure you created?
Why did you leave me like this,
where the failings always outweigh the good intentions bit
when I fail?

God,
I'm at it again.
See me,
this miserable sinner before you?
Why do I always come back like this,
where the confessions always seem greater than the success bit?
See! I've failed.

God,
forgive me again.
See me,
this needy confessor before you?
You know I always need you like this,
when new beginnings are so important, especially in the times
when I fail …

Fourth in Lent

Old Testament: Joshua 5:9-12
Epistle: 2 Corinthians 5:16-21
Gospel: Luke 15:1-3, 11b-32

19 Introductions

Mike enjoyed working in the day centre. He didn't have any qualifications for working with the clients there, but he had shown a natural aptitude for getting alongside the adults with learning difficulties and had fitted in very well indeed. He'd started off just helping out, keeping the place tidy, assisting with serving the lunches, and the like. But now, two years on, he'd graduated to one-to-one work with some of the clients, helping them with specifics in their own programmes of 'activities of daily life'.

He was particularly pleased when the Centre manager asked him one day if he felt confident enough to take Dave, one of his favourite clients, into town as part of his 'extended learning' programme. This was a process whereby clients in the day centre were introduced to activities beyond the safety of the day centre itself and its sympathetic staff. It included using public transport, getting used to money, learning about shopping and using public facilities, as well as exploring all the social skills that went along with these everyday activities.

So the following day Mike and Dave were heading into town. Knowing when the right bus came along, negotiating the correct bus fare and ticket regime, knowing which stop to get off at, were all carried off with ease. Dave had done all of this before. Mike's confidence in his client's ability was high.

The culmination of this particular trip into town was 'Using the Post Office'. Mike had been working with Dave back in the day centre, practising buying stamps and posting letters. Now it was time for the real thing. Mike was confident in Dave's ability. Dave was confident in his own learning. So both client and helper arrived at the town post office in high spirits.

What neither Dave nor Mike was ready for was … The Long

Queue! The post office was packed, with a long queue snaking from the end of the counters to the front door, in and out of looping blue ropes hung from silvery metal stanchions.

Dave wasn't bothered. He strode right up to the nearest counter and boldly announced, 'One first class stamp, please!' There were mutterings in the queue. The counter clerk said firmly, 'You'll have to wait your turn, I'm afraid.' Mike came to the rescue, retrieved the obviously disappointed Dave, and returned with him to the back of the queue. 'Why can't I get my stamp?' Dave asked, loudly enough for the whole post office and half the people in the high street to hear. Mike explained about the queue, and politeness, and patience, and waiting. Dave lapsed into silence, and even the inch-by-inch shuffling forward of the queue, and the occasional mechanical voice announcing, 'Counter number four please,' 'Counter number one please,' didn't seem to help. Dave was bored, and Mike knew that Dave and boredom didn't go together at all well.

He was concerned, therefore, that after five minutes of an inching-forward silence Dave tapped the man in front of him in the queue on the shoulder. 'Excuse me, what's your name?' The business-suited gentleman half turned around. 'I'm sorry?' he replied, clearly irritated. 'What's your name?' Dave enquired again, and, proffering his hand, announced, 'I'm Dave. What are *you* called?'

Mike was embarrassed. '*Dave!*' he whispered to his client, 'You don't do that.' 'I'm sorry,' he said to the business gent, trying his best to stave off any fuss. 'No, no, it's OK,' the man replied, and, looking at Dave, he said, 'Hello, I'm Mr Ch … No, I'm Bill.' And, taking Dave's hand, he shook it firmly, and said, 'How do you do, Dave?' 'I'm very well,' the beaming Dave responded. 'Good to meet you.' Dave turned round and grinned at Mike, clearly delighted with the successful use of his social skills to relieve his boredom. City gent returned to his silence. The queue inched forward.

But Dave wasn't finished. Encouraged by his success in his first getting-to-know-you venture, he thought he'd try his luck further down the queue. So, slipping past his new-found friend, he tapped the woman in front on the shoulder. 'Excuse me, what's your name?' The matronly type half turned around. 'I'm sorry,' she replied, 'were you addressing me?' 'Yes, what's your name?' and, proffering his hand, announced, 'I'm Dave. Who are you?' Before Mike could intervene, offer his apology and rescue this unsuspecting woman from his over-friendly client, the lady smiled disarmingly. 'I'm Mabel.' And, taking Dave's hand, shook it firmly and said, 'How do you do, Dave?' 'I'm very well,' the beaming Dave responded. 'Good to meet you.' And turning back to the bemused city gent, he enquired, 'Bill, have you met Mabel? Mabel, this is Bill.' And, before they knew it, Mabel and Bill were shaking hands, enquiring after each other's welfare, and beaming widely. By the time Dave got to the counter to buy his stamp, a lot of people in that post office queue had shaken hands with people they'd never met before, and no one left the post office without a smile on their face.

Dave bought his stamp without any problem. The letter was posted as per the plan. But Mike reckoned the 'extended learning programme' had extended way beyond the needs of a day centre client, and that a lot of people in that post office queue had learned some very important things for *their* 'activities of daily life'.

A smile

I went home on the bus today.
The only seat I could get
was one of those seats facing the back of the bus,
where you have the whole back row
looking straight at you.
Well,
they might have looked if they'd been bothered.
But you don't have any eye contact on the bus,
do you?

And you certainly never smile.

The matronly type was studying my tie –
intently –
obviously with no great liking for my sartorial elegance,
at least, that's what her face told me,
but she never said,
and I never asked …
For you don't have any eye contact on the bus,
do you?

And the kid with the iPod,
with the ubiquitous white noise
leaking from his headphones …
and the girl with the magazine …
and the man counting the parked cars …
and the lady furiously texting and smiling at her reply
and not at any anyone else …
Well, you don't have any eye contact on the bus,
do you?

And me, doing the same …
not liking the matronly lady's earrings,
and trying to read someone else's magazine
upside down,
and doing my own texting,
and when someone catches me looking,
me looking away …
Because you don't have any eye contact on the bus,
do you?

And a baby comes on in its mother's arms,
and they sit opposite,
and the mother looks down the bus,

and the baby looks around
and catches my eye,
and I smile,
and the baby smiles back,
and the matronly lady catches me smiling,
and she smiles at me,
and I smile back,
and the whole bus journey is transformed.

But you don't have any eye contact on the bus
do you?
And you should certainly never smile.

Fifth in Lent

Old Testament: Isaiah 43:16-21
Epistle: Philippians 3:4b-14
Gospel: John 12:1-8

20 Happiness

Quentin always sat on the same bench in the park. He liked where it was – slightly shaded by the old oak tree; within sight of the duck pond but far enough away not to be disturbed by the squeals of the children; close to a bed of deep-red roses which he enjoyed throughout the summer.

Quentin always sat on the same bench in the park at the same time of day. Every morning after breakfast he would go down to the paper-shop on the corner, exchange greetings with the shop staff, buy his morning paper, walk the short distance to the park, take his place on his favourite bench by 9.30, and spend an hour or so catching up with the news and breaking the back of the cryptic crossword. Sunshine or cold, regular as clockwork, Quentin would be in his place. The only days he didn't venture out were when it was very wet, but then no one was out and about on wet days, so no one would notice his absence from his familiar spot.

Quentin always sat on the same bench in the park at the same time of day, and he usually sat alone. He liked that. Not that he chose to avoid company. It was just because that bench in that place and at that time of day didn't ever appear to be in great demand. It gave Quentin time to himself, time to sit and think, or time just to sit.

Quentin always sat on the same bench in the park at the same time of day. He usually sat alone, and *sometimes* he would think about the inscription on the back of the bench. He'd noticed it the first time he'd found what was to become his favourite place. You couldn't miss it. Unlike all the other benches in the park with their designer plaques, the inscription on Quentin's bench had been hand-carved, in italicised script, deep into the wood, and it read: *Happiness is the Summer of 1973.* Quentin had always been intrigued by the inscription, and from time to time he would run his finger along the lettering, or put his paper down beside him and let his mind wander. What could have happened back in 1973 to make someone so happy? Why would it be so important to mark it in such a prominent way? Who was involved? Was the happiness here or somewhere else? Why did it matter so much to put a bench with this inscription in this place?

Quentin always sat on the same bench in the park at the same time of day. He usually sat alone, and sometimes he would think about the inscription on the back of the bench. Indeed, it was on one of the occasions when he was sitting pondering that someone came to sit beside him. Well, not exactly *beside* him, for social convention dictated that if Quentin was sitting at one end, a new bench-sitter should sit along at the other end as far away as possible so as not to intrude on the other person's space. And that's just what the lady did. She was a slim, well dressed, matronly kind of woman, about Quentin's age (mid-sixties, he reckoned). 'Morning,' she offered politely as she sat down. 'Morning. Fine day,' Quentin responded. That was enough. Silence took over. Quentin returned to his crossword. And the lady sat still and looked vaguely into the distance.

She stayed about ten minutes or so. Then, when she rose to go, Quentin was surprised to see her turn around and run her finger lovingly and carefully along the inscription on the back of the bench. Clearly lost in her own private world, she slowly traced out every letter, every curve, every swirl of the wording. Twice she did that, from one end of the inscription to the other. When she was done, she smiled at Quentin as if noticing him for the first time, and, offering no farewell, turned to go. As she did, Quentin was sure he noticed a tear in her eye.

Quentin always sat on the same bench in the park at the same time of day. He usually sat alone, and sometimes he would think about the inscription on the back of the bench. And when he did, he would think about what had happened in 1973 that mattered so much to a well-dressed, matronly kind of lady, and whether she still knew any of that happiness all these years later.

True happiness

It happened on a Sabbath morn,
Or so the story goes,
When crowds arrived to line the city streets,
And children waved their branches high,
And grown-ups threw their cloaks
Upon the ground, their Saviour King to greet.

And happiness embraced the crowd
As halleluiahs rang,
And passion cries became their welcome prayer.
The time was right, the day was good,
And hearts rejoiced anew,
As praise conveyed a joy beyond compare.

It happened on a summer's day,
Or so the story goes,
When happiness to someone's life was given ...
A peace restored ... a hope renewed ...
A King of Love come close
To offer a transforming glimpse of heaven.

That happiness has had its way,
Not only then, but now,
As halleluiahs ring across the years.
And songs of love, and cries of peace,
Still echo in the heart,
And praises still make laughter out of tears.

It happens on this Sabbath morn,
Or so the story goes,
When crowds arrive to celebrate a day
Of palms and passion, pride and praise,

And cloaks cast on the ground,
As Love is humbly carried on its way.

So come, rejoice! Sings psalms of praise!
Let halleluiahs ring!
Wave palms with joy! Once more a gift is given!
Our peace restored … our hope renewed …
A King of Love brings close
True happiness – another glimpse of heaven.

Passion/Palm Sunday

Old Testament: Isaiah 50:4-9*a*
Epistle: Philippians 2:5-11
Gospel: Luke 22:14-23:46

21 Sceptical

Granny Cameron wasn't an easy lady to like – at least, that was the word on the streets. 'Ferocious,' Drew had heard her called. 'Eats young vicars for breakfast,' he'd been warned.

Father Drew Gardener, newly arrived vicar in the parish, had not yet had the chance to make up his own mind. Granny Cameron had been pointed out to him in church on his first Sunday. He was sure she'd glowered at him as they shook hands at the church door after the service. But he'd not had time to meet her properly. And being an open-minded kind of guy and always prepared to give people the benefit of the doubt, he was sure Granny Cameron couldn't be as bad as people made out.

Mind you, he was conscious of putting off going to visit … Subconsciously believing the street-talk? Doubting his own good will? Sceptical? Who knows … ?

Maybe that's why Father Drew Gardener was a touch apprehensive on a pouring wet Tuesday afternoon as he stood facing the door of Number 27 Lavender Terrace, staring at the tartan nameplate proclaiming that a 'Cameron' lived there. Tentatively, he pressed the bell. A 'bing-bong' sounded somewhere in the distance. Drew waited, getting wetter by the minute. He'd waited long enough to decide that he should pop a visiting card through the letter-box and hot-foot it down the path to the shelter of his car, when the flap of the letter-box suddenly clanged open. Two spectacle-covered eyes were framed in the space, and a disembodied Scottish voice barked, 'Yes? Who is it?'

Drew stooped down and met the staring eyes. 'It's Father Gardener … from the church … the vicar … come to visit …' he stumbled. The response was the snapping shut of the letter-box and the sound of many keys being turned, bolts shifted and chains rattled. After what seemed an eternity, and Drew now sopping wet, the door slowly swung open. 'Well, come in, man, come in … Ah huvnae got a' day …' The increasingly worried Father Gardener had his first welcome to Granny Cameron's abode.

Well … 'welcome' was pushing it a bit! 'Good God, man, yer drippin' a' ower ma guid hall carpet. Tak' yer shoes off. Lay them there, on the lino by the door. No, dinnae hang yer coat there. It'll drip a' ower the wallpaper. Tak' it intae the kitchen, man. Pit it ower a chair. No, dinnae go in there. That's the guid room. Go in yonder. Tak' a seat in ma back room. No, dinnae sit there. Can ye no' see that's ma seat? Sit doon there, on that high-backed chair. Sit doon, man. Dinnae stand there makin' the place look cluttered. Sit doon, man, sit doon.'

Drew had not been brave enough to make any response to this tirade of instructions, other than to do as he was bid at every turn. But what he did know was that, for the first time in his fledgling ministry, he was scared. He'd never been introduced to *this* kind of thing in the Pastoral Care tutorials in Seminary.

He remembers little of that first visit to Granny Cameron's abode – apart from his feeling terrified, *and* the fact that the whole place bore the heavy, pungent scent of Freesia Talc! It was a smell he knew well, an aroma evocative of his great-grandmother's house where he was often taken to visit as a small boy. His mother had told him later what the smell was. From then on it was unmistakable. Whatever else there was to say about Granny Cameron, she was definitely a user – of deep-scented Freesia Talc.

Drew was relieved to get out of *Chez Cameron* with his life, after his grilling about the length of his sermons *and* the length of his hair; whether he had any children *and* whether his wife would be involved with the Mothers' Union; what he thought of homosexuals *and* women priests; and much more besides. In the end he had to agree with the word on the streets - Granny Cameron wasn't an easy lady to like!

That's why he was surprised two days later when he went to the door early in the evening to answer the door-bell, only to find the porch completely empty – apart from a red geranium on the shelf, roughly wrapped in thick, brown paper. Attached to it was a note on which was scribbled in a spidery hand, in pencil, 'Welcome to your new home. I hope you and your lassie will be very happy among us.' And the note was unsigned ...

Drew wasn't a gardening man, and to his untrained eye one geranium looked much like another, though he had a distinct feeling he'd seen this particular red geranium somewhere before. But, for the life of him he couldn't remember where – until, turning round to take his new house-warming present into the shelter of his home, he caught the unmistakable aroma of deep-scented Freesia Talc.

The gift

You may not know me,
But I have something to share ...
You may not like me,
But I have something so rare ...
You may not want me,
But I have something that's new ...
You may not need me,
But I have something for you.

For when you know me,
You'll find the something I share ...
And when you like me,
You'll find the something so rare ...
And when you want me,
You'll find the something that's new ...
And when you need me,
You'll find the something's for you.

So, now you know me,
You'll feel the living I share ...
And when you like me,
You'll find compassion so rare ...
And if you want me,
You'll know commitment that's new ...
I know you'll need me,
So I'll give my loving to you.

Monday of Holy Week

Old Testament: Isaiah 42:1-9
Epistle: Hebrews 9:11-15
Gospel: John 12:1-11

22 Mrs Garrity's Monday morning

Mrs Garrity always enjoyed Monday mornings, especially since she'd taken over the Primary Five class at the beginning of the new term. They were, she was always telling her husband, 'a joy and a delight', the best class she'd ever had. Working with this group of nine-year-olds made teaching a genuine pleasure.

And Mondays? Well, that was the time when the pattern of the week was set. It began with 'conversation time' around what had happened to the children at the weekend. And in the spirit of 'integrated learning' and an 'across the board curriculum' (or whatever the fancy title was *this* year ...) there could be many spin-offs from that first-thing-on-a-Monday session. They'd had geography, culture, national anthems, league-tables, and much more besides, when the children had been excited about the Olympic Games ... They'd had weather maps, skin-care, explorations of deserts, and much more besides, when there had been a long heatwave ... It was always 'conversation time' that started it all off. Mrs Garrity always enjoyed Monday mornings.

This Monday morning was no different. The children were keen to get started – always a good sign. 'Well now, Class 5C, here we are. It's Monday again. It's been *ages* since we were together – two whole days. And I'm sure that *so* much has happened for all of us. So ... who wants to start our "conversation time" this Monday morning?'

Brian had his hand up first. 'Well, Brian, and what's been happening for you this weekend?' Brian dropped his hand onto his lap. The answer came slowly and deliberately. 'Please, Mrs Garrity, my goldfish died on Saturday.' There were sighs of sympathy. Some of the children had obviously heard the sad tale already. 'Please, Miss, Brian's goldfish was called Tigger ...' 'It was swimming upside down in the fish-tank, Miss ...' And out came the whole, sorry story, sometimes from enthusiastic reporters, but mostly from a downcast Brian – the death ... the discovery ... the family arrangements ... the garden funeral ... the tears ... and the promised trip to the pet-shop next Saturday to purchase a suitable replacement ...

'Please, Miss, my Gran's cat died,' Pauline offered when Brian's saga had come to an appropriate conclusion, and another tale unfolded around the sad demise of Pauline's Gran's moggy – 'Kola' the cat rescued as a kitten from the cat and dog home ... seventeen years old ... Gran's fourth cat ... black and white ... bringing mice in from Gran's back yard ... put down by the vet ... promise of a photograph to be brought in later in the week ...

'Please, Miss, Madge died in *Neighbours*,' Emily reminded everyone, and off the class went again – TV Soaps ... Australia ... Harold's tears ... Madge being nice ... why people get sick ... grown-ups who die ...

Through it all there was typical animation, listening, respect, understanding, sympathy, ideas for later in the week, and much more besides ... Yes indeed, another good 'conversation time' on a Monday morning. 'Well, children, I think that's enough for now,' Mrs Garrity suggested, finding a suitable point to draw the session to a close. But Edward Henderson still had his hand up. 'I think we're done, Edward, unless you have anything else to add about goldfish, or cats, or *Neighbours*.' 'No Miss,' Edward replied quietly. 'Well then, unless it's something special, I think we'll move on.' 'It *is* special, Miss,' Edward responded, his voice almost down to a whisper. Mrs Garrity was astute enough to know there was something in Edward Henderson's voice that was different from usual. 'Well, Edward, what is it you want to add?' she enquired.

'Please, Miss, my little brother died.' There was a stunned silence. All the children looked round at Edward Henderson. For a second the teacher of Primary 5C wondered if this was for real. But the look on Edward's face told her it most certainly was. She took a deep breath. 'Do you want to tell us about it, Edward?' And in a quiet but firm voice that's just what Edward Henderson did ... a pregnant mother ... a rush to hospital on Friday night ... an emergency ... a baby called Colin ... machines and tubes ... a little brother's death on Sunday morning ... Granny coming to stay ... a big sister crying ... Edward in hospital seeing his mum ... his dad telling him what had happened ... the family at the house ... Edward feeling sad ...

Mrs Garrity didn't really know what to say. But there was no need for her to worry, for the children of Class 5C did the work for Edward, and they did it well. The children asked appropriate questions, and Edward Henderson talked. Someone wondered when Edward's mum would get home from hospital, and Edward Henderson talked, and talked. There were enquiries about why the baby was sick, and Edward Henderson just talked, and talked, and talked.

'Can I make a card and send it to Edward's mum, Miss? My Gran got cards when "Kola" died, Miss,' piped up Pauline. 'So did Harold in *Neighbours*, Miss,' Emily offered. 'No one gave me a card when my goldfish died,' complained a forlorn Brian. And the tension was broken.

Mrs Garrity kept a watchful eye on Edward as the day went on. But it was clear that the talking and talking and talking had done its job. The children had done the job for Edward Henderson, but Mrs Garrity had lots of ideas for curriculum issues for that week and, indeed, for many weeks to come.

That's why Mrs Garrity always enjoyed Monday mornings, and was always telling her husband that the children of Primary 5C were 'a joy and a delight', the best class she'd ever had.

Death?

'What's death?' they asked.

'It comes to us all,' was the reply.

'Are you sure?' they asked.

'Death's as certain as taxes,' was the reply.

'Why should that be?' they asked.

'Because life is limited,' was the reply.

'Limited by what?' they asked.

'By time,' was the reply.

'Does time run out for everyone?' they asked.

'For everyone, including me and you,' was the reply.

'Is that all?' they asked.

'All of what?' was the reply.

'All of life when time's finished?' they asked.

'I don't think so,' was the reply.

'Is death not the end, then?' they asked.

'I hope not,' was the reply.

'What happens after death, then?' they asked.

'You live,' was the reply.

'Live where?' they asked.

'In love,' was the reply.

'Doesn't love die?' they asked.

'Never, ever,' was the reply.

'Where does love go on?' they asked.

'In you,' was the reply.

'Now?' they asked.

'And for ever,' was the reply.

'And when I die?' they asked.

'Love never dies,' was the reply.

'Will I live on in love?' they asked.

'For ever,' was the reply.

'Is that eternity?' they asked.

'I think so,' was the reply.
'Really?' they asked.
'I hope so,' was the reply.
'What's death?' I asked.
'A kind of interruption in eternity,' they replied.

Tuesday of Holy Week

Old Testament: Isaiah 49:1-7
Epistle: 1 Corinthians 1:18-31
Gospel: John 12:20-36

23 Betrayal

There was no doubt about it, Bobo felt betrayed. As far as he was concerned he'd done nothing amiss, the innocent victim, in the wrong place at the wrong time, done for something he didn't do.

It wasn't that he hadn't been in bother before. Well, Bobo and trouble seemed to attract each other. He'd lost count of the number of times he'd been put out of the classroom, hanging about in the corridor like some leftover from a house removal, standing there, forlorn and useless, with all the other kids filing past on their way to another lesson, and all of them thinking, no doubt, 'There's Bobo in bother again …'

He was well familiar with the inside of the headmaster's office too. When being put out of the class wasn't deemed enough of a punishment, he would be frogmarched by a furious teacher down the corridor to the door that proclaimed that a 'Headmaster' resided here, and left there to face his additional punishment.

Bobo hated 'Hitler', as all the kids in the school had christened Mr Walters, the High School's legendary head teacher. If it wasn't the barking voice, it was the glowering stare … If it wasn't the stamping foot, it was the clipped moustache. What else but 'Hitler' could such a man be called? And Bobo hated this little man with a passion. Of course it was always his own fault. He knew that well enough. For if Bobo and trouble hadn't gone hand in hand for so long and so regularly, he and Mr Walters wouldn't have become so well acquainted. But they had, and Bobo had been at the end of every punishment Mr Walters could mete out, and had experienced every piece of sarcasm, every threat, every put down a recalcitrant kid could imagine.

And yet, despite all of that, the thing that hurt Bobo the most was the betrayal. Sitting in the police station with his mother, it was all he could think about. His mother wasn't saying much. There wasn't much she could say. The police had come to the door in the early hours of the morning and had insisted that Bobo 'accompany them to the station in the furtherance of their enquiries'. His mother had come with him – well, it was an age issue for Bobo – and she had obviously been struck dumb by the whole business.

Bobo wasn't saying much either. But he was thinking plenty. He knew someone had 'grassed him up' to the police. How else could they have known he was with the crowd outside the chip-shop when the gang-fight had started? Gang-fights weren't Bobo's thing. In fact, fighting of any kind was something he would avoid at all costs. But he liked being with the lads, the 'gang', if you like. And that meant 'guilt by association', as the police put it. Yes, he'd been there, right enough, but only because he was sitting on the low wall by the road at the time, wolfing into a fish-supper. He didn't know who started the stuff with the Asian kid. But it had kicked off good and proper. And, when it did, Bobo had legged it. Too much explaining to do if you were still there when the police arrived …

So why had he been lifted? Someone had put his name in the frame. Some rat-bag had done the dirty, and Bobo felt betrayed.

Bobo wasn't in the police station long. No one seemed too concerned to press things with Bobo that much. No doubt the main men had been lifted and Bobo was deemed to be too much of a small-fry to bother with. Some names had been put to him, right enough. But he'd said he'd seen nothing and was too busy with his fish supper to take any notice of who'd done what to whom. There was no way *he* was going to name names. Betrayal just wasn't Bobo's style.

So he'd walked. Actually, he and his mum had got a bus home, neither of them saying much. But Bobo was thinking about betrayal, and wondering whether he needed to do anything about it.

Sorry

God, it's hard to put this into words.
But ... well ... you see ...
I'm sorry.
There! I've said it out loud.
I'm sorry ...
I've let you down.

Actually, I'm not quite sure what that means,
even though I know I'm supposed to see it that way
and believe it, and understand it.
But I'm not exactly sure what letting God down is really about.
Is that betrayal?
I'm just not sure.
Sorry ...

So I'll stick with what I know.
I'm sorry ...
I've let myself down.
All the stuff I promised myself I wouldn't do,
well ... I blew it!
And all the stuff I promised I would do –
you know, the good stuff –
well, not that much of it got done.

I'm sorry ...
I've let other people down as well –
like Charlie, my mate, when I gave him a hard time,
and my sister when I broke my promise,
and Mr Chilcott ... you know ...
I don't have to spell it out, do I?
And all the rest I've let down?
Too long a list, I'm afraid.

So, I'm sorry …
I'm really sorry …
I've let myself down, and I've let other people down.
That's what I know.
So I'm sorry.

And if that means I've let you down too,
then I'm sorry about that as well.
Actually, I'm still not quite sure what that means,
even though I know I'm supposed to see it that way
and believe it, and understand it.

But I'm sorry anyway. OK?

Wednesday of Holy Week

Old Testament: Isaiah 50: 4–9a
Epistle: Hebrews 12: 1–3
Gospel: John 13: 21–32

24 Beyond words

This is the only story in this compilation which is told in the first person. I tell it this way because, although I have tried to depersonalise it, quite simply I can't. So I shall tell it as it happened, and let the story speak for itself.

Josephine was a patient in our hospice. She had been widowed for a number of years and she had no family of her own, her nearest relatives being two devoted nieces. And Josephine hated her name! So she made it clear to all of us on the hospice team that she was not to be called Josephine. Jo was OK; Josie was her preference; and even Mrs Hutton was acceptable if you wanted to be formal. But Josephine? No way, not unless you wanted an earful of complaint.

It was that kind of spirit which endeared Josie (and even writing this, I'd better not incur her wrath by using the wrong name ...) to every one of us on the staff. She was one of our most respected and loved patients. And Josie did well. Her admission to the hospice had been for control of her symptoms and to allow an assessment of what her needs might be to help her return home. Because, although Josie had a life-limiting illness, she wanted and needed to be at home. So for the three weeks of her admission, a lot of work was done so that she could get back to the familiarity of her own surroundings and routine.

In time, her symptoms being better controlled, her assessment completed and equipment and care-services ready for her at home, a date was fixed for her discharge. It was for Josie a successful admission, and though we all knew she would be returning to the hospice when things deteriorated, we were delighted that she was going home.

On the morning of her discharge, the hospice was extremely busy, one of those frenetic periods we have to deal with from time to time. As the chaplain I had become caught up in the busyness and had several rather complex situations to deal with – and all at the same time, it seemed. So, to be honest, I was somewhat irritated when I heard that Josie wanted to see me before she went home – irritated because I had more than enough to do, because I knew that the ambulance would be coming for Josie shortly, and because I'd already shared a farewell with her earlier in the day.

So, out of duty rather than desire I appeared at Josie's bedside. She apologised for bothering me – which put my irritation *firmly* in its place – and took me completely by surprise by asking me if I'd give her Communion before she went home. I was surprised for two reasons: requests for Communion were not common in the hospice; and, as far as I was aware, Josie never went to church. It didn't seem appropriate to enquire about the whys and wherefores of Josie's request, so I arranged to take her to the hospice Quiet Room half-an-hour later for a short Communion service prior to her departure.

When the time came for the Communion and with Josie already there and waiting – her case by her side and her coat over the arm of her chair – the ambulance had already arrived, and two clearly agitated ambulance men were not best pleased at the delay in taking their patient home. So a somewhat frazzled chaplain decided that Communion was going to be short, and I hoped that Josie wasn't going to notice how abbreviated a version she was going to get. Well, after all, she wasn't a church-goer and wasn't likely to be aware of the difference, was she? So, with all the calmness I could muster, Josie and I settled down to our Communion, and I realised to my horror that I had forgotten my Service Book. In my rush to get things organised, I had picked up a prayer book with a similar black cover, and not the Communion Ordinal. It wasn't such a disaster as it might have been, though, for I comforted myself that Josie wouldn't know any better, and that, although I didn't have the words before me, I could remember enough to get by.

I'd only just begun when I realised that Josie was silently mouthing the words of the Communion Service. Clearly and distinctly, she was saying all the words, quietly to herself, word by word, phrase by phrase, section by section. Half way through the dedication prayer, I got stuck – I simply forgot what came next. Josie raised her head from her prayerful pose, smiled sympathetically, and the silent mouthing became a quietly heard repetition of the words of the prayer.

And so it continued, sometimes me, sometimes Josie getting the words of the Communion right. When we were done, I sat for a time in silence. Josie looked at me with a furrowed brow as if there was something I'd missed. Then, realising that the chaplain wasn't going to get it right, she smiled again, looked me in the eye, took me by the hand, and whispered, 'The Lord be with you.' And I dutifully replied, as *her* congregation, 'And also with you.'

Josie had her Communion before she went home. But, who was offering the Sacrament, and who was benefiting from it? Josie may have got the words right, but for me, in that Communion Service, the meaning and significance of it all was beyond words altogether.

This sacramental time

Bread and wine,
set out on a table,
enough for you and me,
and anyone else who might come along.

Wine and bread,
in a cup, on a plate,
the ordinary becoming sacramental,
in the mystery of not knowing how.

Words and thoughts,
set out in a book,

enough for you and me,
and anyone else who might hear these words of invitation too.

Thoughts and words,
never trapped in a book,
but offering now a meaning
beyond words, in the mystery of holy thoughts.

You and me,
round a table of communing,
enough to fill this place
with a congregation of saints and angels.

Me and you,
beckoned to this feast,
enough to fill our souls,
in the wonder of this sacramental time.

Maundy Thursday

Old Testament: Exodus 12:1-14
Epistle: 1 Corinthians 11:23-26
Gospel: John 13:1-17, 31b-35

25 Murdo the storyteller

Murdo always sat at the door of his cottage smoking his pipe. On wet days and in the colder days of winter he would sit just inside his porch. But mostly he sat outside the door, on a rickety bench, wreathed in pipe smoke. Every day for as long as Ian could remember, on his walk to school and on the journey home, Murdo was sitting there. Sometimes he had someone with him, enjoying the chat. Occasionally there would be two or three old men, making more pipe smoke than usual. And from time to time he would be surrounded by a bunch of kids, sitting cross-legged on the ground, under the smiling gaze of passers-by.

Ian remembered the first time he sat with the rest of the kids at Murdo's feet. It was like being in some mystery world – the smile on the craggy face which Ian could now see close up, the white whiskers stained brown, an old-man's hat on his head. For Murdo was a story-teller, and the tales he told, recounted in his slow, deep drawl, were a joy for a young child's ears – about sailing with the herring fleet when he was a young man, huge waves, massive catches, dangerous journeys; about the war, trenches, comrades, dangers, rescues; about poaching, late nights, salmon nets, evading the Laird's men. Ian loved old Murdo, for Murdo was a storyteller.

One day, on his way home from school, Ian noticed that Murdo wasn't in his usual place outside his porch. The door was closed and so were the curtains in his cottage. Ian was puzzled, and when he got home he enquired of his mother where Murdo might be. Mother looked serious. 'That's for your father to tell you,' she whispered, and went back to her household chores. When father came in a little later, Ian was surprised to see him in his Sunday suit and not his working overalls. He and mother had a whispered conversation, and then, looking really solemn, father took Ian by the hand. 'Come with me,' was all he said.

Ian's father led him down the village towards Murdo's cottage. The curtains were still pulled and the door closed. Father knocked and went straight in. The front room was full of people, some of whom Ian knew, many of whom he didn't. There were nods of recognition towards his father and embarrassed smiles at Ian. Still holding the young lad's hand, Ian's father led him through the crowded room and into the back of the cottage. He opened another door and man and boy were in a bedroom, and there was Murdo lying on his back on a big double bed with his clothes on and with his eyes closed, just as if he was sleeping. There was a faint, musty smell - the unmistakable reek of pipe-tobacco. Ian's father took him to the side of the bed, lifted his hand and gently laid his son's open palm on old Murdo's forehead. It was cold. Murdo didn't move - no flickering eyes or twitching moustache or broad smile. Father let Ian keep his hand on Murdo's forehead for a long time. After a while, not knowing what to do next, Ian turned to look at his father, who smiled, and looked serious and wise at the same time - as father often did.

'Murdo is dead,' his father said. 'He died this morning. Take in all that you see here. Fix in your memory all you see and feel in this room. Remember your hand on Murdo's forehead. There is no fear in this place. "In the midst of life there is death" and you need not ever be afraid of death, no matter what others might say. "The Lord giveth and the Lord taketh away. Blessed be the name of the Lord."'

Ian still remembers Murdo, and, in his mind's eye, he can still see him at the door of his cottage, wreathed in pipe-smoke. He can still hear his voice and delight in his stories. And sometimes, when his own grandchildren are around, he tells them some of the stories Murdo told, and the story about Murdo's dying, and some good stories of his own as well.

Ian knows that, one day, he'll die too, and maybe, because of Murdo the storyteller, he'll not be afraid of death when it comes. And maybe he can help the children feel that way as well.

Remembering

Well I remember his living,
The wonder of his presence,
The fullness of his being,
The loving of his life.

Well I remember his dying,
The coldness of his brow,
The stillness of his body,
The departing of his soul.

Well I remember her living,
The countless treasure of memories,
The words of wisdom,
The enduring influence on me.

Well I remember her dying,
The fearfulness of departing,
The hellishness of coping,
The brokenness of grief.

Well I remember their living,
The rejoicing of their faith,
The dignity in the face of mortality,
The fearlessness of letting go.

Well I remember their dying,
Their saintly presence still around,
Their abiding in eternity,
Their constancy with me.

Well I remember your Living,
The cry, 'My beloved',
The stories and the healing,
The meaning and the mystery.

Well I remember your Dying,
The cry 'It is finished',
The laying down in the tomb,
The waiting for eternity to dawn.

Good Friday

Old Testament: Isaiah 52:13-53:12
Epistle: Hebrews 4:14-16; 5:7-9
Gospel: John 18:1-19:42

26 Puzzled

She was puzzled by the single red rose. Greta had noticed it the first time she'd walked past the plot in the far corner of the cemetery. The grave had been newly dug, turf replaced on the turned earth with the expectation that it would knit together and return to its original grassy smoothness. There was no headstone as yet and, indeed, no other floral tributes to cover the grave-site – unlike the two or three other newly used plots still marked with their fading wreaths and dying flowers in torn polythene. This grave was marked by just one delicate red rose.

Greta visited the cemetery every week. She'd done that regularly since Clark had died. At the beginning it had been every day. She just couldn't keep away. She'd have pitched a tent beside his grave and kept a vigil if she could have got away with it. But that's not socially acceptable, is it? Well, not in leafy suburbia anyway, and not when you don't want your family to think you're barking mad. But now, all these years later, it was once a week, her personal vigil-time with Clark.

Greta did most of her thinking in the cemetery. Clark's untimely death had been devastating of course, and there were times when she'd wanted to be dead too, such was the pain of living without the love of her life. But time had restored a perspective, and the journey of living again was beginning to bring its own sense of purpose. But her trips to the cemetery were still important, and the thinking she did there mattered a lot.

She never stopped reminding her children that, once a week, they should walk through a cemetery, not just to be close to their dad, but to remind themselves of the fragility of life and the transience of our time. 'Don't rely on permanence,' she would tell them. 'There's more to life than material things.' They listened, of course, and smiled a lot, and did their own thing – which probably didn't include walking through a cemetery once a week to remind themselves of their mortality. Well, you don't when you're young, do you?

So Greta had her own weekly walk through the cemetery, and her time with Clark, and her thinking. She'd pondered the grave of a city councillor and benefactor beside the resting place of a teenage girl. She'd mused on the great enclosed plot which housed the graves of the Lord of the Manor and his family over many generations and the simple headstone of a devoted local couple. She'd cried many times as she'd stood by the memorial of those who fell in two World Wars and, beside it, the white gravestone of a soldier killed in Afghanistan. Occasionally, she'd watch from a respectful distance as another funeral took place, and sneak a look at the cards on the flowers after the mourners had gone.

And today, Greta was puzzled by the single red rose on the newly dug grave. There was no card with this flower. The vibrant red of its half-opened blossom was in stark contrast to the dirty green of the turf beneath it. The deep green of the few leaves on the stem was only slightly obscured by the plastic of the wrapping.

The single red rose lay on the grave for five weeks. It faded. It withered. It died. But still it lay in its place. Then, one day, the remains of the single red rose had gone, only to be replaced by another one, and, after a few weeks, another, and another, and another. Still no headstone marked the grave, but someone, somewhere, at some time or another, was making their personal pilgrimage, a regular vigil of remembrance, to mark a resting place of a loved one with a single red rose.

Who could this be who came to an unmarked grave and remembered? Someone like her, mourning the loss of a partner? A mother, trying to cope with the loss of a child? A friend, keeping alive the memory of a best mate? A daughter, trying to make sense of the loss of a father? A follower, remembering a leader? A colleague, paying tribute to a pal? A lover, weeping for the loss of a soul-mate? Whoever it was, Greta reckoned she understood, for someone was remembering as they should, and someone, hopefully – unlike her children – was taking time to think of their mortality and the different perspective that might create in their own life …

Greta never knew who came to offer their own personal vigil with the single red rose on the unmarked grave. But it didn't matter. For, whoever it was, they were part of the great company of those who still mourn and remember, a company which Greta knew and understood.

How long?

How often should I come
and stand in silent tribute where you are laid to rest?

What should I say
as I scream silently with all the pain of missing you?
What should I offer now
through much unspoken questioning
of all I do not understand and never will?
What will I voice of raging at your going,
and anger, even now, that I am left behind?
What should I speak of tender love
and all that yet I need to say of what you mean to me?

How long should this go on,
this pilgrimage of sorrow,
this ritual of remembrance,
this vigil of silent mourning?

Will answers come - from you or yet from me?

I do not know…

But what is clear is this –
that on this day, and in this place,
and for this loss,
and in my love for you,
I needs must do what I must do ...

And so I come as often as I must ...
And I'll return as time dictates I should be here ...
And I will speak – or not – as I will be ...
And I'll go on as long as I might need ...
And I will mourn as I still grieve for you ...
And I'll remember now, as then, as I must hold you near ...

This is your resting place;
but I will never rest in my remembrance times,
for this, my pilgrimage,
this, my vigil,
is my gift to you.
For I can do no less but come to where you have been laid,
and remember and be sad,
and remember and give thanks
for all you are and yet will be.

Holy Saturday

Old Testament: Lamentations 3:1-9, 19-24
Epistle: 1 Peter 4:1-8
Gospel: John 19:38-42

27 Janie's long wait

It had been a hard week. Indeed, if she thought about it long enough, Janie would have decided it had been a hard, very hard, month. She'd not been happy when Daniel had to go to Iraq. Not that he *had* to go. No one had twisted an arm up his back. But it had always been a kind of 'Hobson's choice'. He didn't have to go, but he *had* to go, kind of thing.

Security was still pretty dodgy in Iraq after the invasion, and things were unstable to say the least. But Daniel's company had been there before the unrest, and now they were in there pitching with the restoration programme. That's what being employed by an engineering firm with a lot of Middle East contracts was about. You had to go where the work was, and you had to cope with the uncertainty. And Daniel having such a senior position ... well, he just *had* to go.

He hated leaving Janie, of course. He made light of the danger and always laughed off the fear-factor, working on the basis that if you started thinking about these things you wouldn't go anywhere near the place. And, after all, he *had* to go ...

The hardest part for Janie while Daniel was away was the news of the bombings. There was always something – another roadside explosion, a suicide attack, a devastating ambush. But the worst of all was the killing of the two civil engineers. At first the reports were sketchy. But by the time the official news had come through Janie was frantic. After all, hadn't the killings happened in the sector where Daniel's firm was based? She'd convinced herself Daniel was dead.

When she'd found out that he wasn't and that the engineers had been part of another company altogether, she was overwhelmed with relief, and then consumed with guilt because she was pleased that it was someone else who'd lost their life.

She'd heard a week ago that Daniel was coming home, but even that was a mess of misinformation and confusion. The planned return home would be delayed ... Then it wasn't ... A date was set ... Then it was changed ... A flight time was fixed, then the flight was re-routed, and the airline altered, and the arrival time uncertain ... It was all too much.

So it was now or never as Janie drank endless cups of coffee in the airport lounge and watched as passengers from every single London flight streamed through the arrival gates. 'It'll be today, sometime, from London ... we hope ...' was all she'd been told. But 'today' seemed like a year, and the waiting was intolerable, as flight after flight came, and passenger after passenger arrived, and greeting after greeting was exchanged – and still no Daniel.

It had been a hard week, a hard month, and this was the worst day of all. The promise had been made. The expectation had been created. But the deliverance wasn't happening. The return hadn't come about.

It was the last flight of the day. A small knot of people were the only ones left in the arrivals lounge. A couple of student types came through the gate first, then a party of businessmen. A family, obviously back from holiday, were next, followed now by a steady stream of returning travellers. Would he never come? Would he never return?

And then she saw him, tired and weary, but walking, half-running towards her. She ran to him, arms outstretched. She couldn't contain herself, and she didn't care what anyone thought. Her love had come back. Was that not worth some spontaneous expression of joy?

She hugged him and kissed him. He held her face in his hands and said her name, 'Janie', as if for the very first time. He wrapped his arms around her and held her close. She wept openly on his shoulder. He did the same on hers. They held each other for what seemed like hours. The whole world, and the baggage claim, and the other passengers, and the airport staff could wait till they were done. After all, it's not every day your love comes back to you like this.

Easter

God, I don't know what to do with Easter.
I've waited so long …
I don't know what I'm supposed to do,
what to say, how to react.

Spontaneous?
Rejoicing?
Letting myself go?
Celebrate?
Well, it's not me, is it?
O God, I don't know what to do with Easter.

God, I know what Easter does to me.
The waiting is over.
It's the way it was supposed to be,
just like you said – remember?

A surprise?
Joy breaking through?
Death overcome?
Celebration on a plate?
Well, it's your way, isn't it?
Thank God, I know what Easter does to me.

God, what does Easter do for you?
The waiting was worth it.
You knew what was supposed to happen.
even though *we* didn't.

Your victory;
your purpose;

your redemption;
your Love come again.
Well, it was always going to be that way.
O God, how much Easter must do for you.

Easter Day

Old Testament: Psalm 118:1-2
Epistle: Acts 10:34-43
Gospel: John 20:1-18

28 The gate

The gate always creaked. No matter the time of day, the season of the year or the quality of the weather, the gate always creaked. It had creaked for as long as Anne could remember. There had always been talk about getting the oil-can out, but it never happened. The creaking gate was comfortingly familiar, and as she slipped through it from the bottom of her garden onto the pathway up to the woods, it creaked as she opened it and it creaked as she closed it. It was a normal, comforting sound, the gate doing its job.

Anne missed John more than ever, and her daily walk through the woods had been one of her few consolations. But even that seemed to be wearing a bit thin. It was six months since John had died, and she thought she'd been doing so well. And, indeed, anyone who knew her even vaguely would have said the same. She was back at her voluntary work. She could go to church now without breaking down in tears. She was at her Bridge evenings again, and was turned out as smartly as before. Yes, indeed, as far as everyone could see, Anne was doing well.

But Anne knew differently. Things were getting worse rather than better. She'd had plenty to do at the start and felt she was progressing well enough. Of course she'd been upset for ages, and she didn't much like being out of control. So she was pleased when she felt things were getting better. But now it was falling apart again. She wasn't sleeping well. She would break down in tears when she came home after the Bridge Club. She didn't actually like going to church, though no one knew that, even if the discerning person should have realised she never stayed for coffee afterwards. And her daily walk in the woods wasn't doing its job any more either.

For a long time she'd taken her daily walk along the path she and John had walked every day with the dogs, and she would sit on the bench at the viewpoint where they'd shared so many happy times. But recently she just felt an overwhelming sense of sadness as she walked and would regularly sit in tears on the bench and wish John had never died. She'd taken to talking to him and even being angry with him for leaving her behind. Why was this happening to her? Was it all going to pieces? Was she mad? Would it never get better? No one ever said it would be like this.

The gate creaked as she shut it behind her. But this time she didn't begin her walk. She just stood looking at the path, trying to decide whether she could cope with the walk or not. Her mind was in turmoil, and with tears rolling down her face, she couldn't get her thoughts straight. It was only a walk, for goodness' sake, so why was she so scared all of a sudden? It was a time to think of John, wasn't it, so was she being disloyal not being able to go? It was part of her daily routine and people said that was important, so why did she want to go back indoors and never face the world again? She stood, and she wept, and she shook, and she panicked.

She decided not to go. She opened the gate to go back home. The gate creaked. But she didn't step through it into the garden. She just listened to it creak. She closed it again. It creaked. She opened it. It creaked. Back and forwards, open and shut, the gate creaked, and creaked, and creaked again, with its familiar, comforting sound.

If anyone had seen her, they would have definitely thought she'd gone mad, as she stood in tears for ages and ages, opening and shutting a gate and listening to it creak.

Then Anne began to realise what was happening. In a strange way, she was listening to the gate for a reason, and she was trying to figure out what it had to say. So what was it saying? 'Open me – and I creak … close me, and I creak …' it began. 'Open, close, creak, creak …' it continued. But as the rhythmic sound of the gate deepened her thoughts, the gate was saying much more: 'Open, close … open, close … creak, creak … creak, creak … come, go … in, out … creak, creak … good, bad … start, finish … creak, creak … keep, going … move,

on ... creak, creak ... hear, me ... life, choice ... creak, creak ...
don't, stop ... start, again ... creak, creak ... creak, creak ...'

Anne couldn't remember how long she'd stood there listening to
the gate. But she gave it one last creak, fastened the catch, turned on
her heel, and started off up the path to the bench at the viewpoint
beyond the woods.

Clarity

It would be nice,
just now and again,
if clarity could come,
right when I need it.
That's what prayer is about,
isn't it?
I pray ...
You respond ...
And everything's clear ...
So why don't I find clarity when I need it,
eh?

It would be nice,
just now and again ...

So, if not big chunks of clarity,
what then?
Little signs?
Small indications?
Tiny, creaky voices?

Oh, well ...
I'll just have to be more aware of those, then,
if that's the way of it,

and find your clarity in bits and pieces
when it comes,
and I need clarity the most,
eh?

First after Easter

Old Testament: Psalm 118:14-29
Epistle: Revelation 1:4-8
Gospel: John 20:19-31

29 Billy's box

Billy had always kept his box in the cupboard beside his bed. It had been there for as long as he could remember. His mum told him once that she'd 'started it' not long after he was born. But now it was his own box, and always had been. And Billy's box was very special indeed.

It was a light-coloured, wooden box with a hinged lid. Billy remembered his dad saying it was a 'seegar-box' – or something of the sort. It had once had a label on the outside, but that had long since gone. Now, emblazoned on the lid in big, red, childish letters – Billy knew he could write much better than that now, but he didn't want to change things – were the words 'BILLYS BOX' (And, no, he didn't know about apostrophes, then or now!)

There was no lock on Billy's box, so he made sure it was kept at the back of his cupboard, well out of sight and away from prying eyes. For Billy's box contained lots of things that mattered to Billy and weren't for anyone else to see.

There were a few things his mum had put there – the name-band Billy had worn in the hospital where he was born, whose faded letters told him he was once called 'Baby Chapman'; and in a little plastic bag a lock of Billy's blond hair from his first hair-cut. But most of the things he'd put there himself because they seemed to matter - the wobbly tooth that had come out in bed one morning; the photo of him and the other kids in his nursery class; a bottle-top he'd found in the garden with a star on it that he'd once used as a sheriff's badge; an old-watch-with-no-strap-that-didn't-go-any-more that he'd got from his grandpa; a 'silver sixpence' that was very old that he'd been given by his gran; a pencil with a Mickey Mouse rubber that he'd liked as soon as he'd seen it; the picture he'd drawn of his mum, with the huge head and sticky-out arms and legs, and with the yellow hair he loved so much. Yes, indeed, Billy's box was special.

When Billy heard his grandpa had died, he went to his room and cried. He wasn't sure why he was crying but it seemed the right thing to do. The grown-ups had been crying a lot, and his mum was crying all the time when she'd told Billy and his little brother that grandpa was dead. 'I wonder what being dead is like,' Billy had thought, but didn't like to say so, because the grown-ups didn't look to be in the kind of mood to answer lots of children's questions. He knew it meant that no one would see grandpa again, and that's why the grown-ups were sad. So he felt sad as well.

When the sad bit was finished for now and the tears had stopped, Billy wondered what he was supposed to do next. He didn't much feel like going downstairs to be with the others. So he did what he always did when he didn't know what to do – he pulled out his box from the back of his bedside cupboard. He rummaged as usual, seeing what treasure in his box should be looked at first. And his fingers fell on the old-watch-with-no-strap-that-didn't-go-any-more he'd got from his grandpa.

Billy took the watch carefully from the box and laid it on the palm of his hand. He looked at it, and then he turned it over again and again, examining it from every side and angle. He felt it tenderly, running his thumb over the glass face, turning the broken winder with his fingers, feeling the pointy-out bits of the bars that had once held the strap. He looked at the time, the big hand on II and the little hand on IX, just as they had always been. And he thought about his grandpa.

He thought about the day grandpa had given him the watch and how grown up he had felt as he placed the treasured gift in his pocket and added it to his box's collection when he'd got home.

He thought about grandpa in his big chair, with his mug of tea and his cheery grin.

He thought about his stories about playing football when he was young - 'I once got a trial with Chelsea', he'd been delighted to recall.

He thought about his bus conductor cap badge - from his first job, he'd said – with its blue lettering in its silver frame.

He thought about what it was like when grandpa hadn't shaved, and he'd hold Billy close to his chin and rub his bristles across his cheek – horrible but nice at the same time.

He thought about grandpa's laugh when they watched 'Tom and Jerry' cartoons together.

He thought of him and gran dancing after the Christmas lunch, across the lounge carpet, grandpa red in the face and gran insisting he stop his nonsense at once, and them both collapsing on the sofa in fits of giggles.

As he turned the watch over and over in his hand, he thought about grandpa being gone for good. But, somehow, grandpa didn't seem to have gone at all. He was there, in his thoughts, very much alive, because of the old-watch-with-no-strap-that-didn't-go-any-more that he got from his grandpa, that would be kept for ever in Billy's box.

Connections

I knew a lady once who fell out with her psychiatrist.
She'd been widowed for eighteen months,
and he was giving her a hard time
because she still had her husband's toothbrush beside hers
in the rack in the bathroom.
'You're stuck in your grief,' he'd said.
'You're not letting him go.'
And she'd told him to stop talking nonsense,
and that perhaps he should see a good psychiatrist!
The bathroom had always had
a red toothbrush and a blue toothbrush
together in the rack above the wash-hand basin,
and it wouldn't be the same if one of them wasn't there.
And anyway,

the red toothbrush reminded her of her husband,
and that was important,
because she still needed to be connected to him
now he was gone.
She wouldn't have it any other way.

I heard a story once
about a bunch of disciples
that other people thought were completely mad,
and gave them a hard time into the bargain,
because they talked about sharing fish and bread on a lakeside shore
with someone who was dead.
'You're stuck in your fantasy,' they said.
'You're not letting him go.'
And they told their doubters to stop talking nonsense.
Their lives had always had fish and bread,
together, shared with their friend,
and life wouldn't be the same
if they didn't share it with him now.
And anyway,
in the sharing he was there,
on a lakeside shore,
eating bread and fish with them.
And that was important,
because they still needed to be connected to him
when others thought he had gone.
And they wouldn't have it any other way.

Second after Easter

Old Testament: Psalm 30
Epistle: Acts 9:1–20
Gospel: John 21:1–19

30 Duncan

Duncan was a shepherd. He lived in a little cottage a few miles out-side the village, in the lee of the rolling hills where the sheep grazed. Winter and summer, in rain and shine, Duncan tended his sheep. At lambing time he would work all hours. At market time he would work all hours. In fact, he seemed to work all hours most of the time. For Duncan loved his work, and Duncan was a good shepherd.

Duncan was in church every Sunday. He would walk to church with his two dogs – which would wait obediently for him at the church door until the worship was over – and take his place with the small congregation. Wearing his tweed suit and plus-fours, a crisp white shirt and tartan tie, he always carried a full-length shepherd's crook, which, so people said, he'd made himself. Taking his seat, he would carefully place the crook under the pew, to be retrieved when it was time to leave.

Cammy thought Duncan the shepherd was just marvellous. At the end of church, when the grown-ups were talking grown-up stuff, Duncan would let Cammy pat his dogs. (It seemed to Cammy that he was the only one Duncan allowed to do that, and it made him feel very grown up indeed.) Sometimes Duncan and Cammy would walk home to Cammy's house, two dogs obediently by their side, and with Cammy's mum and dad following a fair distance behind. That made Cammy feel even more grown up, and even though Duncan said very little, Cammy just adored his company. And when Duncan left him to walk with his dogs towards the hills, Cammy would wave him goodbye till he was out of sight.

One day when they were leaving the church gate ready for their grown-up journey home, Duncan turned to Cammy, and in his gentle, lilting voice, said, 'Well, young laddie, would you like to hold this and see us safely on our way?', and held out his precious shepherd's crook. Cammy couldn't speak. He took the revered object in his hand and began to stride for home. It took him a few steps before he got the rhythm right, for the crook was bigger than he was. But he soon got the hang of it.

All too soon they were at Cammy's gate. Duncan looked down at the young boy and smiled. 'Aye, laddie, you look the part. You'll make a good shepherd yourself one day.' And, with the precious crook returned to the hands of its rightful owner, Duncan headed for the hills once again. Walking with Duncan was special. Walking with Duncan's shepherd's crook was the best ever.

One Sunday Cammy came out of church and there were no dogs. He waited, and there was no Duncan. His mum and dad told him it was time to go home. 'But where's Duncan?' he asked. His parents looked at each other as if not knowing what to say. It seemed like ages. Then, his father bent down towards him and said in a hushed tone, 'Duncan'll not be back, son.' 'Why? Where's he gone? What's happened?' 'Duncan's gone to be with God,' said Cammy's dad. 'He was old, and that's what happens when you're old. C'mon, son, let's go home.' And, holding hands between his mum and dad, that's what Cammy did.

Cammy had lots of questions. Gone-to-be-with-God was one of them. He knew if it was about God it would be OK. But where was God, and where was Duncan, and why had Duncan chosen to go with God and not stay with them, and what happened to his dogs, and where was his shepherd's crook?

Later in the week, before he went off to school, Cammy saw his father putting on his Sunday suit and wearing a black tie. Now he knew. Duncan was dead. That's what grown-ups do when someone's dead. (Why hadn't his dad just said that?) Cammy didn't cry. He just thought about Duncan, and walking home from church, and playing with the dogs, and holding the shepherd's crook, and he felt good inside.

When Cammy came home from school that afternoon there was a familiar shepherd's crook leaning against the back gate of his house.

Cammy ran inside. 'Mum! Dad! Is Duncan here? Has Duncan come back from God?' His parents looked surprised. 'No,' his mum replied, 'no, son, he hasn't … he can't … you see …' His dad interrupted. 'Why, son? Why do you think that?' 'The crook, Duncan's crook,' blurted the breathless Cammy. 'It's down by the gate.'

Soon all three were in the garden to investigate. And, sure enough, the shepherd's crook was where Cammy said it would be. His father took it carefully in his hands. 'Look,' he whispered, 'there's a label attached to the horn handle.' 'What's it say, dad?' Cammy asked, increasingly enthused by the mystery.

There was a long silence. 'It's from Duncan's son,' his dad began. Another long silence. 'What's it say, what's it say?' Cammy pressed impatiently, almost bursting with excitement. 'It's addressed to you, son,' said his dad. And he read: 'Cammy. This is for you. It was my father's favourite thing in all the world. He would want you to have it. He told me you'd make a good shepherd yourself one day, and a good shepherd needs a good shepherd's crook.'

★ ★ ★

Cammy is a shepherd. He goes to church every Sunday and carefully places his shepherd's crook under his pew, and retrieves it for the journey home. There's always a wee boy patting his dogs when he comes out of church, and he enjoys walking home with the little lad, though they don't say much. The wee fella looks right grown up.

One Sunday, before they set off home, Cammy bends down to his young companion. 'Well, young laddie, would you like to hold this and see us safely on our way?' and places a revered shepherd's crook in the hands of a proud youngster. Cammy smiles to himself as he watches the lad struggle to get the rhythm right with a crook bigger than himself. But, pretty soon, it's just fine.

'Aye, laddie, you look the part. You'll make a good shepherd your-self one day …' he hears Duncan whisper in his ear.

Shepherds

The Lord is my shepherd ...
I know that.
It's an image I like,
of tenderness and awareness,
of leading and following,
of protection and permanence,
and all directed to me.
I like that.
The Lord is my shepherd ...
a shepherd for me.

The Lord gives me shepherds ...
I know that.
It's an image I like,
of parenting and friendship,
of role-models and examples,
of love shown and standards kept high,
and all to benefit me.
I like that.
The Lord gives me shepherds ...
shepherds for me.

The Lord makes me a shepherd ...
I know that.
It's an image I like,
of time and commitment,
of talents and attitude,
of loving and healing,
and all called forth from me.
I like that.
The Lord makes me a shepherd ...
A shepherd ... That's me.

Third after Easter

Old Testament: Psalm 23
Epistle: Revelation 7:9-17
Gospel: John 10:22-30

31 A friend in Id

For Jawad, Ramadan was always a special time of year. Still being a teenager, he'd only been obligated to follow all the appropriate religious customs for a couple of years. But he loved it, and felt very grown up when such an important time came round.

At the beginning of this year's Ramadan, the ninth month in the Islamic calendar, he'd climbed with family to the top of the house to catch a first sight of the new moon. Once it had been sighted, he'd come down into the house with the family, they'd prayed together and then ate their *Suhur*, the early morning meal of bread, mutton and pancakes. Then the fasting began, from dawn till dusk, and that's when Jawad had felt truly at peace with himself and at one with his family and his religion.

Every evening during Ramadan, when the sun had set, he'd gathered with his family round the dinner table, broken his fast with them by eating a single date and having a sip of water, and then left the table to pray, returning afterwards to finish the evening meal, their *afar*, together.

And, of course, he looked forward to Id al-Fitr, or 'Id' [pronounced *Eed*] as it was commonly known, not just because the end of Ramadan was the time to break the fast, decorate the house and exchange gifts with relatives, but because it was the culmination of such an important season.

When Id arrived, all the family went to the Mosque as was the custom, and came home afterwards to a time of celebration, preparations having been under way for some days, with anticipation rising as Ramadan drew to its conclusion. Jawad always enjoyed the Id party in the evening, with the plentiful supply of sweet foods and soft drinks, especially *Sekanjabin,* the sweet mint drink his grandmother always made. But on this particular evening of Id, Jawad was more thoughtful than usual. In fact, if he was honest, he was quite disturbed in himself.

It had begun on the way home from the Mosque. The family, walking together, were chatting as usual and, a little bit behind, Jawad was responsible for his two younger brothers. As they'd rounded a corner, they'd almost stumbled over an old man slumped in a shop doorway with his feet sticking out onto the pavement and a mangy, mongrel dog lying by his side. The old man had a straggly white beard and deep-lined, leathery skin, and he wore a greasy black hat. He was dressed in torn trousers and a dirty gabardine raincoat tied at the waist with string, and his toes were sticking out through the splits in his shoes.

Jawad was taken by surprise at such a sight, for he'd never seen the likes before, and he and his two brothers just stopped and stared. The old man took off his greasy hat, revealing an almost bald head which appeared to be covered in sores. Holding the hat out to the three boys, he muttered in a croaky voice, 'Any spare change for an old man?' Before Jawad could think of replying, he was conscious of his mother appearing by his side. 'Come, Jawad, Rafan, Walif. Come now! Do not spend your time with such a creature. Come! Leave him now! Quickly! Quickly!'

'But ...' Jawad began. 'You must come! Hurry now!' his mother ordered and, taking the two younger boys by the hand, ushered her three offspring out of sight of the old beggar.

Jawad was disturbed. The 'But ...' lingered in his mind. He was too good a son to question his mother's wisdom and disobey her clear instruction. But he could not forget the old man in the shop doorway. After all, wasn't giving alms to the poor just as important as everything else in Id? And wasn't an old man in a shop doorway one of the poor?

During the evening party, Jawad could not get the sad old man out of his mind. So he decided to do something which, if discovered, would, at worst, displease his mother, and, at best, leave him with some explaining to do. But he decided ... Allah's way was more important ...

So, with the party in full swing, he quietly gathered up some of the sweetmeats in a plastic bag and slipped out of the back door of his home. Within moments he was turning the corner into the street where the old beggar had sat. And there he found him, seemingly not having moved from his begging spot.

Jawad knelt down beside him. The old man looked up without a word. Jawad didn't know what to say, so he simply held out the plastic bag, dropped it gently into the old man's lap, and whispered, 'It's Id. So I want to share this with you.' The old man offered no response, but thrusting his hand gingerly into the bag he unearthed one of the sweet cakes and, not even pausing to examine it, stuffed it eagerly into his mouth.

Jawad's job was done, and, leaving the poor man to wolf down the remaining Id sweetmeats ravenously, he hurried home. He hadn't been missed. The party had a while yet to run. The tables were still filled with goodies. But Jawad wasn't disturbed any more. And, unnoticed, he slipped upstairs and began his prayers, remembering with satisfaction that Jawad, his own name, meant 'generous' and 'open-handed'.

A new commandment

A new commandment, you said …

A *new* commandment?
But what's new about loving people?
Isn't that enshrined in all moral codes,
and hasn't it been a truth people have lived by,
a principle that's held humanity together
from the beginning of time?

A *new* commandment?
Really?

A new commandment, you said ...

But, then again, you may be right;
for we kind of got it a bit wrong, didn't we?
After all, if we'd loved one another
since the beginning of time
then we wouldn't have had so many wars
and created so much chaos, would we?

A new commandment, you said ...

I suppose what's *new*, as you put it,
is you, showing what real love is about.
That's what you mean, isn't it?
It isn't abstract any more,
just morality, codes to live by,
vague ideas, and the like.

A new commandment, you said ...

To love as you loved;
to live as you lived;
to show that we know where Love comes from;
putting love into practice,
showing it matters, all the time,
by who we are and what we do, and things like that.

A new commandment, you said ...

OK, OK, I hear you ...
It's about loving like it matters,
like it is *new*, and important,
the most important thing of all;

it's about living *in* love …
That *is* new, isn't it?

A new commandment, you said …

A *new* commandment …
Really!!

Fourth after Easter

Old Testament: Psalm 148
Epistle: Acts 11:1-18
Gospel: John 13:31-35

32 Monkey

Monkey was an ex-boxer – and, as you might have guessed, his real name wasn't 'Monkey'. It was cruel, but Monkey had been the victim of his unfortunate tag for as long as people could remember.

No one could recall his real name, or, if they did, no one ever used it. For Monkey had a face that had seen a few beatings in its time, and with his battered countenance, his loping gait and his slurred speech, the Monkey label had stuck. And, to make matters worse, years ago Monkey had damaged his brain at the boxing.

He'd never been a very good boxer, and as a result he'd taken too many punches and been counted out too many times. Monkey had been slow and not too bright, but big and naturally strong. He'd 'proved' himself in some amateur stuff when the local fair had come to town. He'd been taken 'under the wing' of a shady promoter, hawked around travelling shows, battered more than he should have been, and then dropped when he could no longer pull in even the smallest of crowds. So now Monkey was an ex-boxer with an ex-brain and an ex-life.

It would be nice to report that, despite his unfortunate nickname, everyone loved this big, amiable character and was full of sympathy for what he had become. But the truth was Monkey wasn't loved. He was still big, but he wasn't amiable. His gruff, intimidating presence made him, at best, someone to be avoided, at worst, someone to be downright scared of.

Not that there was any proof that Monkey had done anything untoward. But who needed proof when rumours abounded? 'Did time …' 'Watch your kids …' 'Not to be crossed …' 'Flies off the handle …' 'Dangerous bugger …' were common whispers when Monkey's name came up. Monkey didn't socialise much. And no sleep was lost over that.

No one could believe it, therefore, when Monkey turned up at the anti-war march. The publicity had done its job. The crowds were gathering in the village square, more than anyone could have expected. On a bright, spring day, protest was the name of the game, and placards, banners and megaphone-encouraged chants gave voice to the anti-war sentiments. Clergy and politicians were at the forefront. There were families and green groups, young people and old, church folk and communists – and Monkey.

Monkey! What on earth was *he* doing here? Word went round. 'He probably doesn't know ...' 'Wrong place, wrong time ...' 'Never gets it right ...' 'Thick as a short plank ...' 'Daft so-and-so ...' 'Someone should tell him ...' But no one did, no one dared, for Monkey was not to be tangled with – no way.

Everything was ready. The clock on the church tower showed 11am, the designated time for the start of the protest. The town brass band was in position at the head of the procession, and the bandmaster was just about to give the signal for the band to strike up, indicating to the assembled crowd that the march was about to move off ... when Monkey was seen striding to the front. People weren't quite pushed out of the way as he moved purposefully to the head of the march, but the crowd certainly parted like a mini Red Sea as Monkey headed forward.

No one knew what was happening. The startled bandmaster had a sudden fear that Monkey had a hatred of brass-band music, and that he was going to scatter the band members and their instruments in a furious outburst before they could even sound a note. He needn't have worried. It wasn't the band that was the object of Monkey's attention.

For, within moments, the big man had got himself in between the back of the band and the marchers at the head of the procession, elbowing his way between the chair of the local CND group and the parish priest. They looked surprised, and were even more taken aback when Monkey grabbed the pole, one end of the leading banner held aloft by the local councillor and the MP.

'Mine!' grunted Monkey. 'Mine to carry.' The councillor wasn't about to argue. He knew Monkey by reputation. So he let go of the banner's pole into Monkey's big hand and shuffled quickly to the side, happy to lose himself in the crowd. For the priest, however, it was different. He knew Monkey in person and had no truck with ill-founded reputations. He moved across to where Monkey was holding the banner higher than ever a five-foot-six councillor could ever aspire to. 'OK, Monkey?' he enquired. Monkey never replied. With one hand still holding the banner – and only Monkey could have done that single-handed – he moved the other hand to his face. He placed his forefinger vertically across both lips as a clear signal to the priest to say no more. Then, with his finger still erect, he raised his hand and pointed upwards to the banner. The priest followed the pointing finger and read the words on the banner for the first time. "Make peace, not war" it proclaimed.

His eyes moved back to Monkey, who now had both hands on the banner pole, and there were great big tears streaming down Monkey's face as the band struck up and the anti-war march moved off.

War

And war –
what think you now of war,
now that these images of death and devastation
are yours to see?

What think you now,
when scenes of war invade your very home,
and disturb the private peacefulness you seek?

Will you still turn away in face of this assault
upon your cherished and well-earned comfort,

and thus ignore the bodies
in the rubble of a ruined town?

Will you avert your gaze
from this portrayal of the screaming child
lying prostrate on the body of a slaughtered mother
outside their bomb-scarred home?

Will you pretend it doesn't matter as image follows image,
and words are heaped on words,
as yet another correspondent
offers up the reasons why it should be so?

Or will you weep with me,
and break your heart at wars like this?

Will you allow your tears to flow,
not in the privacy of your secret thoughts,
but here and now,
even for the scrutiny
of the wondering gaze of those nearby,
so that they might ask, 'Why are you upset?'
and find their answer in the scenes of war
and your response?

And will you pledge yourself to work for peace,
to cry for justice and reconciliation?

What think you now of war
when what was far away and in another place
is close and happening now,
when those who died who did not belong to you
now reach out to you
in pain and hopelessness?

What think you now,
when you are broken too,
and weep, and rage, and scream
at this assault on your own precious, peaceful life?

Fifth after Easter

Old Testament: Psalm 67
Epistle: Revelation 21:22-22:5
Gospel: John 14:23-29

33 Invisible to the eye

Trudy was blind. She hadn't been blind from birth, but she'd had to cope with an increasing deterioration in her sight over the years as a result of her diabetes. For a time it had been manageable and she'd still been able to get out and about. But in recent months she'd lost the little sight she'd had left and was now totally blind.

She was all right at home, and with the familiar layout of her little flat and a lot of good advice from caring and sensitive professionals, she was managing pretty well. Occasionally she would venture out, but only in the company of a sighted friend. She didn't like being so vulnerable and dependent and, in time, she would have liked to be more self-sufficient. But not yet. A solo trip out would have to wait. Trudy wasn't worried about that, for she had enough to do to get used to things at home. And anyway, Trudy had always been a very contented lady.

The thing she missed most, though, was the Lunch Club at the Community Centre. She'd always enjoyed the company and the nice people who ran it. And it had meant that, twice a week, she didn't have to worry about cooking for herself. Maybe she'd get back there eventually, once she'd built up her confidence. But for now, ready-meals would have to suffice.

Jennifer was the organiser of things like that. She was, Trudy never tired of saying, a lifeline, and much to Jennifer's embarrassment Trudy would tell anyone who cared to listen that she just wouldn't have been able to manage without her 'angel' Jennifer. Social Services had come up trumps when they'd asked Jennifer to be Trudy's key worker. Angels come in many guises …

That's why Jennifer and Trudy were together one wet Monday evening catching up on how the weekend had gone and what Trudy's plans and needs were for the week ahead. It was Jennifer's final visit of the day and she always enjoyed calling in on Trudy before she went home. The light was already fading by the time she arrived at Trudy's flat, but the flat was well lit and, having greeted her friend at the front door, within moments Trudy was sitting with Jennifer in the sitting room, and the two of them were chatting in their usual animated fashion.

They were only a few minutes into the conversation when the power-cut happened. Well, it *may* have been a power-cut, or it could have been that the bulb in the sitting room light had blown, or maybe the electricity meter in Trudy's flat hadn't been topped up sufficiently. But, whatever the cause of the loss of power, Jennifer and Trudy were sitting in total darkness.

Jennifer knew that. She couldn't see her hand in front of her face. But it took her a few moments to realise that Trudy had no idea they were sitting in darkness. Trudy had been in the middle of a long story and, despite the loss of light, she hadn't missed a beat. Simply put, she had no idea the lights had gone out.

Jennifer wondered if she should say anything, but she didn't want to interrupt Trudy's story or to cause her any alarm. So she sat on in darkness and carried on with her supportive conversation. She wondered how she would manage stumbling to the door when it was time to leave. She smiled when she realised that she might have to ask Trudy for help – a bit of a turn-around in their relationship.

Trudy must have picked up something in Jennifer's voice. For, a few minutes later, she paused in her story, and asked, 'Is there something wrong, dear? You're not yourself.' Jennifer laughed. 'Sorry, Trudy. But we've been sitting in darkness for the past few minutes. All the lights have gone out. I can't see a thing!' 'Oh, dearie, dearie me. You should have said, my love. I was just going to top up the meter with my power-card before you arrived. Wait you there. I'll go and get it sorted.'

Jennifer was just about to offer to do it for her, but she didn't. After all, she had no idea where the meter was or how to do the necessary. And the whole place was pitch-black. So she sat still for a moment while Trudy sorted things out. The lights came on. Trudy returned. She and Jennifer laughed at their – or at least Jennifer's – misfortune.

Soon it was time for Jennifer to leave. Trudy saw her friend to the front door. They parted with their usual hug. But before Jennifer went on her way down the stair, Trudy held her by the hand. 'It must have been funny, dear, sitting in darkness, especially when I didn't notice. But, you see, I don't see things like you do any more. What matters to me can't be seen. Maybe that should be the same for all of us, my dear. What *really* matters is invisible to sight. Even in my darkness, I see so much that matters.'

Trudy squeezed Jennifer's hand. Jennifer smiled at her friend. Trudy smiled back – as if responding to a smile she could see as clear as day!

Remember

Remember me, when by your side I stood
In silent presence, there to wait with you.
Remember me, just as you said you would.
And in the presence I'll be there with you.

Remember me, when by your side I walked
On steady journeys, there to go with you.
Remember me, recalling how we talked.
And on each journey I'll be there with you.

Remember me, when you would take my hand
In tender sharing, to be joined with you.
Remember me, reliving what we planned.
And in the sharing I'll be there with you.

Remember me, when time is hard to fill,
In lonely waiting, no one there with you.
Remember me, when bonds continue still.
In constant loving I'll be there with you.

Remember me, when I'm beyond your sight,
In blinded seeing, never there for you.
Remember me, and see with inner eye.
Invisible no longer, I'll be there with you

Remember me, when you will search the skies
In constant wonder. Am I gone from you?
Remember me in all your tears and sighs,
And hear my promise – I'm still one with you.

Ascension Day

Old Testament: Psalm 47
Epistle: Acts 1:1-11
Gospel: Luke 24:44-53

34 Through clouds and sunshine

Charles had always loved working out what pictures he could see in the clouds. It was a fascinating pastime which he had learned in the company of his grandma many years before, when, as a small boy, he would spend much of the school holidays in his grandma's cottage by the sea. He'd always thought of it as *grandma's* cottage. But, of course, grandfather lived there too. Charles didn't care for his grandfather very much. He was quite a nice man and always gave Charles a great welcome at the beginning of the holidays. But what he *didn't* like about grandfather was that he'd been a teacher – a *head*-teacher, he never tired of telling everyone - and, even though he'd been retired for some time, he didn't seem able to leave his teaching behind – especially with Charles.

Everything, it seemed, could be readily turned into a lesson. Broccoli on the plate for dinner (grandma *always* encouraged Charles to eat his greens) and Charles was subjected to a lesson on horticulture, and how broccoli was related to the brussels sprout (euch!), and how they'd both originated from the wild cabbage, and so on and so forth … Charles fascinated by the clarity of the night sky, and off grandfather would go with a treatise on planetary motion, and the names of constellations, and how many miles were in a light-year, and on and on … Charles having to play indoors when it was raining, and grandfather seizing the opportunity to offer a lecture on prevailing winds, and isobars, and the effect of the Gulf Stream, and much more besides … It wasn't that Charles didn't *want* to learn. It's just that he didn't want to be learning *all the time.* But it was just grandfather's way, and Charles, being a good boy, listened with patience and said thank you.

Grandma was quite different. She always seemed to be more able to take things at Charles' pace. She would ask *him* questions about what he saw, and how he felt, and what he liked, and how he was

154 A blessing to follow

working things out. And she always seemed to have lots of time for Charles. The thing Charles liked doing most with grandma was going for walks by the shore. Now, if it had been with grandfather, walks by the shore would have been nature lessons, or an opportunity to compare molluscs, or explain wave motion. But with grandma walks were mostly in silence, holding hands, feeling the wind in your face, and kicking up the soft sand with your bare feet. And best of all was trying to work out what pictures you could see in the clouds.

'What can you see in the clouds today?' grandma would ask, breaking a long, companionable silence. And Charles would look up for a while and then exclaim, 'Look, grandma, there's a dragon over there, being chased by three pigeons, and a man with a big stick ...' And grandma would laugh and say that all she saw was a giant meringue and several snowballs, and the walk would continue in silence for a time. Then, when the wind had sufficiently altered the clouds so that new patterns had emerged, she would ask again, 'What can you see in the clouds now, Charles?' and off Charles would go on another flight of fancy, with descriptions of wizards, or mountain ranges, or saxophone-players, or giant butterflies. For what Charles saw in the clouds was what he saw. And grandma liked that.

Years later, Charles could still sense grandma's affirmation when he looked into a cloudy sky. Indeed, when he was stressed, he would go outside and try to work out what pictures he could see in the clouds, and finding horses chasing a cabbage or a crocodile with a bow-tie always seemed to make the world a more relaxed place. And when he was weighed down with responsibilities, finding patterns in the clouds never failed to bring out that childlike part of him and restore a kind of balance. And, of course, it always reminded him of grandma, and that was never a bad thing.

One day Charles was sitting at a corner table in the office canteen staring out of the window – needing to work on some cloud pictures – when one of his colleagues sat down beside him. 'Some interesting cloud formations today, don't you think?' the new companion offered. 'Wow!' thought Charles, 'Another sensible guy who's learned from his grandma how to find pictures in the clouds - and I never knew.' And he was just about to offer what he could see, when his colleague continued … 'Actually, that formation over there is a cumulonimbus. Did you know that a cumulonimbus is a type of cloud that is involved in thunderstorms and other intense weather systems? Really it's a result of atmospheric instability. These clouds can form alone, in clusters, or along a cold front in a squall line. They usually form from cumulus clouds at a much lower height, making them grow vertically instead of horizontally, thus giving the cumulonimbus its typical mushroom shape.'

Charles smiled. 'Thank you,' he said. 'That's very helpful. *I* was going to say that what I could see in the clouds today was a fat lady wearing a large crinoline dress, carrying a fancy parasol, and with a Pekinese dog under her left arm. But it's too late now. She's gone.' And, with that, Charles left his by now silent and bemused colleague at the corner table and went on his way, pausing only to glance out of the window to see his grandma winking at him from the clouds.

I see

I see what I see
And I know what I know.
I see what has been revealed
And I know what I should always have known –
That I see what I see
And I know what I know,
And I feel good about that.

Seventh after Easter

Old Testament: Psalm 97
Epistle: Acts 16:16-34
Gospel: John 17:20-26

35 One over the eight

George and Harry were two old characters who shared a ward during their time in the hospice. In the evenings, once the visitors had gone, they would settle in the lounge to watch the TV, especially if there was sport on the box. Football was the great thing. George was a fan of one city team, and Harry a fan of the other. Conversations could become heated, but the humour was always good. At their time of life there were some things that remained much more important than even life and death.

One evening, with the two old boys ensconced in their favourite armchairs in the hospice lounge, one of the nurses asked them if they would like a wee dram before they went to bed. It wasn't an unusual occurrence - 'For medicinal purposes,' the doctor had said. Their reply was instantaneous, and within minutes George and Harry were toasting each other with a glass of Single Malt. Over the next hour or so, as another football match unfolded, the nurse looked in several times, and, finding the two of them still sipping on their whisky, left them in peace. Contentment reigned. Other patients were asleep. Two old men were enjoying each other's company, with a football match on the telly, and a wee whisky. All was right with the world.

When the game was over and the two fans had exchanged their strong opinions on the result, Harry got up to go to bed – and promptly fell over. Big panic! Nurses came running. Harry was helped to his feet and checked over – nothing broken, thankfully – and was taken to bed. Once settled, he was out like a light - and no need for sleeping pills either! George was the same, and the two old boys snored to their hearts' content – best night's sleep in ages. Harry roused the next morning with a terrible headache. George was no better. After declining breakfast, the two of them spent the rest of the morning in their beds. The nurses were puzzled.

The mystery was solved later in the morning when the ward domestic found an empty whisky bottle down the back cushions of the sofa in the TV lounge. No one knew where it had come from. But the ward doctor had a fair idea …

Intrigued, the young doctor had some time in the ward later in the day and was curious to find out how the events of the past 24 hours actually fitted together. Harry and George were back in the lounge, sipping large mugs of tea and looking, for such normally bold lads, somewhat sheepish. 'Good game last night?' the doctor enquired. 'Not too bad, Doc,' said Harry. 'Good night had by all?' 'The best!' Harry smiled. 'But we've been found out,' chimed in George from across the lounge. 'Oh, and how was that?' the doctor probed, keen to encourage the conversation

'Have you no' heard o' the empty bottle the cleanin' lassie found this mornin'?' The doctor looked suitably quizzical and tried not to betray his insider knowledge with the hint of a smile. It mattered little. For George was on a roll.

'Well,' he continued, 'it may have been empty this mornin', but it was full last night. Harry's laddie had a win on the horses and he sneaked a bottle in for Harry an' masel'. And yon wee dram the nurses thought was the same one a' the time had been filled and emptied half a dozen times till the bottle was done. It was the best night me and Harry have had for ages. I was one over the eight, and Harry was even worse than me. Eh, Harry?' 'Aye, right enough, a rare night,' Harry replied, 'an' well blessed by the spirit …'

Two old men laughed uproariously at their antics, and a doctor laughed at an unexpected sign of the human spirit – and not just the Single Malt kind! And three friends laughed in the face of mortality, because, after all, there *are* some things that are more important than life and death, aren't there?

Pentecost

Fire and wind, noise and smoke ...
Frightened men with boldness spoke
Words that all could understand,
Going out where none had planned
On Pentecost.

Tongues of flame, a rushing gale ...
Women too, no longer frail,
Taking out, through street and square,
Breaking news to all found there
At Pentecost.

Spirit of the living God
Fill us as we spread abroad
Words of truth at your command,
So that all might understand
This Pentecost.

God of spirit, wind and fire,
Comforter, our souls inspire.
Real excitement fills the air,
Light and life beyond compare –
Our Pentecost.

Pentecost

Old Testament: Psalm 104:24-35
Epistle: Acts 2:1-21
Gospel: John 14:8-17, 25-27

36 The milking-stool

Johnny's granny had been a milkmaid. Not recently, of course, for Johnny's granny was a *very* old lady. But Johnny's granny had been a milkmaid, ages and *ages* ago, when she was not much older than Johnny was now - so she delighted in telling him. For Johnny just loved it when his granny told him stories about 'the olden days', like when she had been a milkmaid, ages and ages ago.

Johnny never really understood much about his granny being a milkmaid till he had been on a visit to a farm with his school class. To be honest, he wasn't that interested up till then. He knew that milkmaid and 'granny when she was young' went together, but not much more. But the visit to the farm had changed all that. It had been so *fascinating*. He'd watched in awe as the farmer got those big, mucky cows into the shed and steered them into their proper places for the milking. His eyes had nearly popped out of his head when he'd seen the men washing the rubbery udders – disgusting and amazing at the same time. He'd been riveted when the big suction tubes were fitted on the udder of each cow. He'd been mesmerised by the rhythmic swish-swish-swish as the milk was squirted into the glass vats.

Johnny couldn't wait to get home to tell his granny that he'd seen what she'd done as a milkmaid in the olden days. And tell her he did, in breathless excitement, in minute detail. Johnny's granny listened with rapt attention, only speaking when Johnny needed a bit of encouragement to explain things in proper order, rather than galloping on too fast with his story. In time, the whole story of the visit to the farm was done. But Johnny wasn't finished yet. He had lots of questions for his granny.

'Did you work on a farm like that in the olden days, granny?' The old lady smiled. 'Well, nearly like that. But it was a long time ago, and things were very different then.'

'Did you have to get the cows into the shed like the farmer did, granny?' 'No,' she replied, 'and it was called a byre in my day. No, son, your grandad did that. It was his job. He was a dairyman, and he looked after the cows, fed them, and things like that. He got them into the byre, and I did the milkin'.'

'Did you have to fit the rubber pipes on to the cows, granny?' Johnny's granny laughed. 'No, laddie, we had no machines like that back then. We had to do it all by hand.'

Johnny wrinkled his nose and furrowed his brow. 'By hand, granny? Do you mean you had to get the milk out of the cows' … eh … thingies … with your *hands*?'

Granny laughed again. 'Aye, I did that. And hard work it was too. One hand on one teat, and one on the other, pulling on one, then on the next, making sure the milk got down into the bucket and none got spilled. And then working with the other two teats, until the bucket was full or the cow was done.'

It was Johnny's turn to listen with rapt attention. 'Bucket, granny, what do you mean? Didn't you have a glass churn like the farmer? Why would you use a bucket?'

'Because that's what you did. A white bucket, galvanised, we called it. And when the bucket was full the milk was tipped into a big metal churn. We had to do it all by hand. No machines then. I spent half my life under a cow, sitting on my three-legged stool.'

This was getting more than enough for Johnny. 'Stool, granny, what's a stool?' 'A stool, son, is a wee seat with three legs, just at the right height to get you in the right place for the milkin'.'

'*Three* legs, granny? Not four like our chairs?'

'No, Johnny, it had to be three. It was perfect for the uneven floor of the byre, don't you see? Four would have been too wobbly. Two? Well, I would just have fallen over. But three was perfect for a milkin' stool, just perfect …'

Johnny had had enough for now. His head was swimming with

the information about granny being a milkmaid in the olden days, and not having machines, and sitting on a three-legged stool, and *everything* ... So he slipped off his granny's knee and went away to process his learning - ancient and modern.

He'd left his granny smiling, not just in recollection of the olden days, and the smell of the byre, and the feel of the milking, and the swish-swish-swish of the milk in the bucket, and the handsome dairyman she'd had her eye on for ages. But she was smiling to herself about how she'd described the three-legged stool, four legs was too many, two legs wasn't enough, one leg and it wasn't a stool at all. But three legs? Her seat for the milking with three legs, each one important, so that a milking-stool could work on an uneven floor. A three-legged stool for the milking. Three legs together ... Perfect, just perfect.

Trinity

Trinities of things,
Repetitive and compelling –
Abraham, Isaac and Jacob;
The Way, the Truth and the Life;
Faith, Hope and Charity;
One Church, one Faith, one Baptism –
Holding together,
A three-way tie;
Any two not surviving without the other.

Is God like that –
Father, Son and Holy Spirit;
Creator, Redeemer and Sustainer;
Or whatever –
Repetitive and compelling;

Holding together,
A three-way tie;
Any two not surviving without the other?

Or should I be happy with the whole
And not worry about the different parts,
As long as I can sit properly on a wobbly floor
And not fall over.

Trinity

Old Testament: Proverbs 8:1-4, 22-31
Epistle: Romans 5:1-5
Gospel: John 16:12-15

37 New life

There was a sense of death around the day centre that wet Tuesday morning in June. Madge had noticed it as soon as she'd arrived. She hadn't been looking forward to coming this week, well, not after Edna had died. For when she and the rest of the Tuesday crowd had been told the previous week that Edna hadn't recovered from her heart attack and had died in the hospital a few days later, a pall of gloom had descended on them all. And now Madge was having to come to the day centre again and look at Edna's empty chair and not have fun with her old friend and the Tuesday crowd any more.

So there was definitely a sense of death around when she arrived. The deadness in her right arm didn't help, of course. And 'dead' was the way she felt about it. She'd never got any real movement back in it since her stroke, and the damned arm was just a dead thing hanging from her shoulder. She kept losing it down the side of the chair. One minute her arm would be there, on the cushion where the carer had put it, and the next it was gone, having slipped down unnoticed between the cushion and the arm of the chair, or hanging down by the side.

No one was in good form that wet Tuesday morning. The staff and volunteers tried their best, of course, but Madge didn't feel much like joining in the reminiscence session, or responding to the quiz questions. Even the bingo failed to lift her spirits – despite one of the staff shouting 'house' for her and brightly telling her she was the proud winner of a tin of lavender talc! Yeuch!

It hit rock bottom when Bridie arrived. It's not that Madge didn't like Bridie, it's just that she wasn't in the mood for her that particular wet Tuesday morning. Bridie was one of the volunteers, a Downs syndrome lass from the local special needs school, who was on a kind of 'work experience' placement in the day centre. She helped with the teas and gave out the quiz sheets, that kind of thing. She was nice, but kind of loud, and Madge simply couldn't be bothered with her today. Nor could Alice, or Chrissie, or Eva, or any one of the Tuesday crowd. Madge could see that. And Bridie probably sensed it too, for she wasn't getting her usual rapport with anyone.

Bridie was, therefore, totally bored, and decided to take herself over to the piano. Now, the piano in the day centre wasn't a great piano. The battered old upright had been donated years before when someone was moving into sheltered housing, and it hadn't been played since, and had really become a piece of old furniture in the corner of the room. There it stood, the lid firmly down, the top a convenient shelf for a bundle of old magazines, a pink geranium that had seen better days, and a red-footed, yellow chicken-thing that had been left there following the Easter celebrations, a rather worn stuffed bird whose better days were, like the piano itself, well in the past.

Gingerly Bridie lifted the piano lid and gently touched one of the keys – 'Plonnnkkk!' – as if she was just checking it was a real piano. Then, pulling over a chair from the table beside her, she sat down and got ready to play. 'Good grief,' muttered Eva, loud enough for anyone to hear, 'this is *all* we need.' 'Noise, noise and more bloody noise, that's all we'll get now,' responded Alice.

Bridie took no heed. Carefully she placed the index finger of her right hand on a white note, took a big deep breath, and, slowly but clearly, with one finger, she started to play … 'Twin - kle - twin - kle - lit - tle - star - how - I - won - der - what - you - are …' from the start right through to the finish.

It was going well, and was *actually* passably pleasant, Madge thought, when … Well, maybe it was because Bridie's success had increased her confidence and she was banging the notes a bit harder, or maybe there was a draft of wind, or maybe it was divine providence, but, all of a sudden, the red-footed, yellow chicken-thing slipped off its perch on the top of the piano and landed with a discernible 'thump' on the budding maestro's piano-playing hand.

Bridie jumped up with a squeal. The chair clattered backwards. The pink geranium fell to its ultimate demise down the back of the piano. The nose of the red-footed, yellow chicken-thing had a go at ending Bridie's new party-piece with an out-of-tune C sharp. And the bold Chrissie shouted with glee, 'Ah ha! There you go! Even yon red-footed, yellow chicken-thing doesn't like your piano-playin'!'

It could all have gone horribly wrong. But it didn't. Instead, Bridie started to giggle, a squeaky, high-pitched kind of giggle. And that started Madge off something terrible. She dissolved into paroxysms of laughter. Her dead arm had long-since disappeared as she clutched her tummy with her good arm. That started Eva off, then Alice, then Chrissie, and soon everyone was in tears of laughter. The staff came in to see what all the rumpus was about. And all they could see was a bunch of old ladies helpless with laughter, and Bridie squeaking above them all, and a red-footed, yellow chicken-thing lying forlornly on the piano keys.

There had been a sense of death around the day centre that wet Tuesday morning in June. But when Madge went home later that day, she was grinning from ear to ear. Somehow she'd found some new life again, and so had the Tuesday crowd, and so had Bridie – and a red-footed, yellow chicken-thing seemed to have found a life of its own as well.

To find new life

God,
I want him back,
no longer dead, no longer gone from me.
My heart is broken for ever
with his departure.
Tell me it is just for a time.
Take me through this pretence of loss,
that I might know it is unreal,

as unreal as I hope it to be,
and find normality again
with his return.

God,
he will not come back;
for he is dead, for ever gone from me.
My heart, so broken at his departure,
tells me it is not for a time;
that this is no pretence of loss;
that this is real,
and reality has to be lived with.
Will I find normality again
if he never returns?

My love,
You cannot have him back;
for death now ends his life, and he is gone from you.
Your broken heart will heal,
though not for a time.
So, do not pretend about this loss.
Be real, and in reality
hold your love close for eternity.
And in that normality you will find new life,
forever bound with him.

Tenth Sunday after Easter

Old Testament: 1 Kings 17:8-24
Epistle: Galatians 1:11-24
Gospel: Luke 7:11-17

38 Velda's shoes

Velda always wore red shoes. Well, not *always*, not for the whole of her life, anyway. But anyone who'd known her in recent times would tell you that they had never seen her wear anything on her feet other than red shoes!

Her slippers were red – a winey kind of red, right enough, dark and scuffed with age, but red, none the less. She had a battered old pair of 'baffies', as she called them, everyday kind of shoes, pretty grubby now, but they'd once been shiny red. And some special people had seen her wearing her sparkling red evening shoes, the high-heeled, pointy-toed ones with sequins on the straps. 'I used to wear these at "the jiggin'",' she'd told her doctor who'd admired her remarkable footwear during one of his house-call visits, 'but it's mair than ma life's worth to wear them for ony length o' time noo, for a micht fa' an' break ma ankle, and then whaur wid ah be?'

So, it appeared, Velda always wore red shoes. And no one knew why … Until, that is, she landed up in hospital.

Velda had fallen and broken her hip. It had happened, she'd explained to a bemused clerkess when she was being admitted to the ward, during a break in the final of the World Snooker Championship on the TV (her favourite programme of all time, she pronounced … such fine, upstanding young men, so well turned out, and no one stepping out of line …). 'Ah got up to go to the kitchen to make a cup o' tea,' she'd recounted, 'an' ma leg got tangled wi' the zimmer leg, an' the zimmer leg got tangled wi' the table leg, an' ah didnae ken which leg tae move first, so ah fell ower!' *'The fact that you were wearing high-heeled dancing shoes too, silly old bat, wouldn't have helped much either,'* mused the clerkess, though she didn't feel she needed to state the obvious. And the red shoes? In the plastic bag by the side of the bed with the rest of the clothes Velda had come in with, ready to be taken home.

Velda never got home. She never recovered. A rapid onset of pneumonia proved resistant to antibiotics, and 'the old person's friend' took her quickly. Death was mercifully peaceful.

It was Velda's only niece who had the responsibility of making the arrangements for Velda's funeral. 'You'll no' need to worry, hen,' she'd told her niece some months before. 'A' the details, an' a' the important bits an' pieces are in a big broon env'lope, in the tap drawer o' yon dresser. It's a' there. You'll need naethin' else.' And she was right – birth certificate, pre-paid funeral plan, will ... It was, indeed, 'all there' as promised – including a detailed letter in Velda's distinctive hand, outlining the details of her funeral service. The hymns, music, Bible readings, a favourite poem, her choice of crematorium, were all carefully detailed. Nothing, it appeared, had been left to chance.

But it was the final part of Velda's letter that was for her niece both the most surprising and the most important. This is how it read ...

'... and I've to be laid in my coffin wearing my red shoes – any pair will do, you can choose. But, if it's possible, I'd really prefer the best of them, my red dancing shoes. You want to know why? Well, I'll tell you ... When I was young, our family was poor and there were no luxuries in our house. One day, in town with my mother, I saw a pair of red dancing shoes in a shop window. I was *so* excited. They were beyond my reach, physically and financially, of course. But I had never been so excited before. There and then, I resolved that *one* day I would have a pair of shoes like that. It took me years. But when I got my first pair of red shoes, I couldn't contain my excitement. To be honest, I never felt more alive than when I had red shoes on my feet. I didn't wear red shoes *all* the time, of course. When I was a teacher, it wasn't done. I would have been laughed out of the school! And the church? Much too ostentatious for those old fogies, don't you think? But for me, at home – and sometimes going out on special occasions – well, my red shoes were my symbol of living, of being the best I could be, of really, *really* being me. So, when I die, I want to be laid out wearing my red shoes. For then I will be fully alive. I'll still be me! And I might even go dancing into eternity and meet my Maker, and hear him say 'Great! Here's Velda on top form, come to give me her all! She's giving me the best that she can be!'

On the day of the funeral, the Order of Service didn't have a picture of Velda on the front as people expected. Instead, the cover was resplendent with a photograph of a pair of sparkling red dancing shoes, high-heeled, pointy-toed ones with sequins on the straps. There was a lot of discussion afterwards about why an Order of Service for a 97-year-old woman should have red shoes on the cover. Everyone had a view. Some folk got it wrong. Others thought it strange. A few got close to the truth. But only a smiling niece knew what it really meant – in eternity Velda was still very much alive, and, at that very moment, was dancing into the Kingdom, being for her God the Velda she was always meant to be.

My all

> She gave you her ointment; she gave you her all;
> Not one little droplet, enough to enthral;
> Not one tiny fraction while keeping the rest …
> She promised she'd give you the best.

> I'll give you what's precious before it's all gone;
> Not what I can spare you when I'm put upon;
> Not when it costs nothing or when I'm too stressed …
> I promise to give you my best.

> She gave you her perfume, her love to fulfil;
> Not just for a moment, performing a drill;
> Not what she could manage, a passing request …
> She promised she'd give you the best.

I'll give you my serving, and not hold things back;
Not just when it suits me to make up the slack;
Not when it's an extra, or when I need blessed ...
I promise to give you my best.

Eleventh Sunday

Old Testament: 1 Kings 21:1-21*a*
Epistle: Galatians 2:15-21
Gospel: Luke 7:36-8:3

39 Graffiti

The graffiti on the wall of the church was seven feet high and stretched along the whole side of the building. It was all the more graphic because of the whitewashed walls, and boldly proclaimed 'Baz Lives. Baz Rules.'

Who on earth Baz was and why he had to use the side of the church to announce his presence was beyond Judy as she took in the newly discovered graffiti. All she knew was that 'Baz' had passed by this way sometime during the hours of darkness, paused to do a bit of spontaneous ecclesiastical decorating, was about six feet tall, and had a penchant for the use of royal blue spray-paint.

Judy wasn't unfamiliar with graffiti in the area. In fact she would have to admit that she actually *liked* some of it, especially the more colourful stuff on the warehouses at the edge of the industrial estate. Indeed, as a local youth worker she was aware of a 'Street Artistry' project that was running in the local school, a constructive attempt to channel budding artistic skill into more creative activities, for some of these spray-painters clearly had a *lot* of talent. But this was just wanton vandalism! A church which had offered a youth café, club nights, a junior football team, trips away, and much more besides – and *this* is the thanks you get.

She was leaning on the fence bemoaning the state of the world when her reverie was interrupted by a bunch of passing teenagers. She knew them all, as they were involved with the church youth-work activities in one way or another. They stopped, and one by one they joined her leaning on the fence.

'I see Baz's out,' one lad commented. 'Still alive, too,' offered another. 'Back to ruling the roost again,' suggested a third.

'Who's Baz?' Judy asked no one in particular. 'Baz?' a number of them said in chorus. 'Baz?' one of them continued. 'You've never

172 A blessing to follow

heard of Baz?' There was knowing laughter from the rest. 'Baz's been doing time … banged up … six months for house-breaking … out last weekend … back to his old tricks … and there's his announcement – Baz Lives. Baz Rules. It was always his line. Tough luck about the church wall, though. Shame …' And with that, they were off, leaving Judy to her increasingly depressing reverie and wondering about the presence in the area of the Mighty Baz.

'Oh well, needs must,' she murmured, and headed down the road to the local DIY store to buy yet another couple of gallons of whitewash and some new brushes. She'd always believed that graffiti should be dealt with right away, to create at least an impression that standards weren't going to be allowed to drop in the face of mindless vandalism. But all she'd ever had to deal with up to now was pretty low-level crime, or, at least, low-level graffiti, the kind you could deal with from ground level. But what on *earth* was she going to do with the seven-foot high stuff, when she could never hope to reach the top of that!

On the way out of the DIY store she bumped into Spanner – literally. 'For f★★★'s sake, watch where you're going, woman! You nearly had me on the ground.' Spanner was a nanosecond away from fisticuffs with his clumsy companion when he realised who it was. 'God, Judy, you were nearly for it there. You should be more careful. And anyway, where are you off to? Looks like you've bought the whole shop?'

Spanner and Judy were old friends, ever since Judy had given a reference for him at Court and had promised to work with him when he did his time. Actually, he never did any time inside, but she'd been a key person in his development through his Community Service Order and the start of his recent apprenticeship. Spanner – and Judy had never enquired as to the origins of such an original name – listened intently as Judy unfolded her tale of woe. 'Baz's out' she began. 'Baz?' Spanner replied. 'He's left a seven-foot-high calling card,' she continued, and went on to explain the graffiti on the church wall. 'Hence the DIY purchases. What a bummer, eh Spanner?' 'More than a bummer,' Spanner offered, 'more than a bummer,' more to himself than to Judy. 'Listen,' he continued, 'give me that stuff and I'll get it sorted.' And before Judy had time to protest, Spanner had relieved her of her bags of paint and brushes and was off up the street.

It was a couple of hours before Judy was back to the church, but when she got there, there wasn't a sign of the graffiti. And standing looking at a newly whitewashed wall was Spanner and the bunch of teenagers she'd spoken with earlier. Spanner saw her coming. 'There ye go!' he chirped. 'Good as new and some of your whitewash left over too.' 'Brilliant!' Judy responded, genuinely amazed at the trans-formation. 'Thanks, Spanner. Thanks lads. You've done a great job.' 'Naw,' came Spanner's retort, 'Naw. That wisnae us. Was it, lads?' There was knowing laughter. 'Well, who?' 'You've never met Baz before, have you?' Spanner pulled a lad, a six-foot, gangly lad, new to Judy, into the centre of the group. 'Baz, this is Judy. Judy, this is Baz.' 'Ah'm sorry, missus,' the clearly sheepish Baz offered his new companion, 'ah cannae shake yer haund. See, ma haunds are still covered wi' a' this white paint.'

There was laughter all round. Judy held out her hand. 'Let me shake your hand anyway, Baz,' she said, 'for any friend of Spanner's is a friend of mine.'

To face the demons

Do I have demons?
Yes I do …
Demons that whisper 'Failed again …'
and make me feel more worthless;
demons I overhear saying, 'No one likes you …'
and I believe what they say;

demons that suggest, 'Your faith's no use to you …'
and I wonder if they're right;
demons that criticise by offering, 'You've not done enough …'
and drive me to busyness I can't cope with;
demons that proclaim, 'It's a bloody disaster …'
and I sink deeper into despair.

Can I name the demons?
Yes I can …
You, who say I've failed …
You're the teacher that said 98% wasn't good enough.
I know you …
You, who say no one likes me …
You're the kid in the playground who laughed at my spots.
I know you …
You, who say my faith's no use …
You're the minister who told me I wasn't a good enough Christian.
I know you …
You, who say I've not done enough …
You're my parents who kept saying
'The devil finds work for idle hands …'
I know you …
You, who say it's a disaster …
You're the God who expects me to be perfect
and never to have doubts.
I know you …

Will I face my demons?
Yes I will …
Begone, demon of failure!
98% means I've done really well.
Depart, demon of self-doubt!
I'm much more than just my spots.

Away with you, demon who undermines faith!
'Even if it's as small as a mustard seed …' someone once said.
Out, out, demon of overwork!
What use will I be if work makes me dead?
I banish you, demon of despair!
This gloom will pass, and I'll still have hope.

Will my demons come back?
Of course, of course.
So to the demon of failure, speak of success.
To the demon of self-doubt, tell of someone who loves you.
To the demon who undermines faith,
offer what you believe of God with you.
To the demon of overwork, show how you can be still.
To the demon of despair, offer your smile of hopefulness.

Oh, didn't I tell you?
Even my demons can be singled out,
named,
shamed,
disarmed,
laughed at,
defeated,
banished …
Just like that …

Twelfth Sunday

Old Testament: 1 Kings 19:1-15*a*
Epistle: Galatians 3:23-29
Gospel: Luke 8:26-39

40 Larry's jacket

Rosemary wondered whether she should be wearing Larry's jacket. Not that anyone ever saw her, for she only wore it indoors or when she was scuttling quickly into the garden to leave the refuse bin by the gate. She would never *dream* of wearing the jacket where people could *see* her. They would think she was barking mad.

In actual fact, Rosemary had begun to wonder herself whether she was more than a little disturbed. After all, wearing your husband's jacket was a *bit* mad, wasn't it? Especially around the house, doing the chores, or making the tea, or watching the TV, *and* with the central heating on as well. And sometimes, she was ashamed to admit, she even wore Larry's jacket instead of a dressing gown when she was going for a bath. Maybe that made her *completely* mad.

She couldn't remember when she'd started wearing Larry's jacket. She seemed to have been doing it since the beginning, but she couldn't recall when that beginning was. The early days had been filled with people and busyness. But people had started to drift away … Well, it happens, doesn't it? Maybe it was when she had to be on her own, really on her own, that she'd started wearing Larry's jacket. The house was so *dreadfully* empty without him. She'd lost count of the number of times she'd thought she'd heard him on the stairs, and broken down in tears when she realised he wasn't there. She'd catch herself thinking she'd tell him some local news when he got in from work, then hated the realisation that he wouldn't be coming home, and ended up in tears again. And how often had she turned to him in the middle of 'The X Factor' or 'Fame Academy' to comment on a performance, only to be faced with his empty chair, and more tears, and more struggles with loneliness – for the umpteenth time.

Whenever it had started, she'd been wearing Larry's jacket for a long time. She wasn't even sure why it was *this* jacket in particular. It certainly wasn't his best one. Most of Larry's good clothes had gone to the local charity shop. That had taken a while to get round to. She'd told the family she'd do it in her own time, and she'd eventually felt strong enough to get it organised. She'd cried buckets while she was doing it, and there were several times when she'd abandoned it altogether – the suit he'd bought for Sarah's wedding; the jumper no one had liked but Larry; the shirt that Larry never liked but everyone else thought was trendy; the sports jacket he'd bought in a sale that was too small so that it had never been worn ... Oh, it was just too much to bear.

She'd kept some things, of course. Well, putting everything out was like throwing him away completely. And she didn't want to do *that*. So she'd kept his jacket, his old green jacket, the one she'd told him should have been thrown out long ago. But she'd been so glad he'd not thrown it out. For somehow the jacket was Larry, and when she wore it she felt as close to him as she could possibly be. And sometimes, when she was wearing Larry's jacket and held her arms tight across her chest, she could feel she was hugging Larry and he was cuddling her, and she felt safe and secure again. Wearing Larry's jacket just seemed right. 'So what if I'm more than a little mad,' she would say, 'that's between me and you, isn't it Larry?' and she would pull the jacket around her a little tighter.

Rosemary didn't really want to go to the Finlaysons' daughter's wedding. But, as Rosemary and Larry's next-door neighbours for many years, Jack and Frances had been such a support and were really good friends. And their only daughter had been in school with Rosemary's eldest. So Rosemary had been persuaded. Her heart wasn't in it. It was her first big 'do' without Larry. But she took it as a challenge that had to be faced.

She'd cried through most of the wedding, but by the time she'd got to the meal and had been warmed by a dry sherry and a glass of good champagne, she'd started to relax a little. Rosemary had been put at the kind of 'odds and sods' table common at weddings – folk from here and there that are single, or non-family, or not-really-close friends. And she was pleased that the woman beside her was pleasant company. As it turned out, she was widowed too, and this was her first 'outing' without her husband. So a lot of good talking was shared. Rosemary could honestly say that she'd enjoyed the wedding more than she'd ever expected to, and the two women continued to appreciate each other's company throughout the evening.

When it came time to go, the sharing of a taxi was arranged and the two women headed home. Rosemary's companion was to be dropped off first. They'd sorted out the shared expense of the cab fare and exchanged phone numbers with the promise to keep in touch, and were just taking their leave of each other when the woman turned to Rosemary and smiled, saying, 'I can't wait to get inside to wear Bert's jacket. It's as if he'll be welcoming me home.' And with that she was gone, and the taxi was taking Rosemary on to her own place.

Rosemary wore Larry's jacket when she was getting ready for bed that night. She told Larry all about the wedding. She told him she'd cried because he wasn't there. She told him she loved him. She told him about a new friend going home to wear her husband's jacket. And she told him she didn't feel she was mad after all, as she pulled Larry's jacket more tightly around her.

I wonder how I'll manage

I wonder how I'll manage in the processes of change,
As I contemplate what's steady and what must be rearranged;
When I feel a bit bewildered, and I don't know why or how …
I wonder how I'm managing just now.

I wonder how I'll manage – or perhaps I'm going mad
As I ride the roller-coaster of the bad, then good, then bad;
When I feel I'm coping better, then the whole world turns to grey …
I wonder how I'm managing today.

I wonder how I'll manage on those special days again,
As I cope with celebrations, but I can't get past the pain;
When I put a happy face on, then it soon will disappear ...
I wonder how I'm managing this year.

I wonder how I'll manage as the time goes on and on,
As I lay a new foundation to build future dreams upon;
When I know it will be different, but just how I've not a clue ...
I wonder how I'm managing what's new.

Yes, I wonder how I'll manage ... so I'll go on wondering still
As I ask 'Can I go forward?', then I answer, 'Yes I will!'
When I know the future's out there, a new picture to be drawn ...
Yes, I wonder how I'll manage;
Yes, I'm going to have to manage;
So I'm trying hard to manage moving on.

Thirteenth Sunday

Old Testament: 2 Kings 2:1-2, 6-14
Epistle: Galatians 5:1, 13-25
Gospel: Luke 9:51-62

41 Seventy-two

It was mid-January, 1972, and John was still living at number 72 Laburnum Avenue. It was a small area of the town known locally as 'The Trees' – Acacia Terrace, Cherry Tree Grove, Laburnum Avenue, that kind of thing. John had lived in Laburnum Avenue since he and his wife, Jean, had been the first occupants seven years ago. It was to be their retirement home, but it hadn't been much of a retirement. Jean had died a year after they'd moved in, and John had been in deteriorating health ever since. 'It's this damned Arthur-itis,' he would complain to anyone who was prepared to listen.

John had few callers at number 72. He and Jean had never had any family and both were only children themselves. So there weren't any family to come around. His carers were good, though - the morning ones, to get him up and washed and dressed; the lunchtime one, to make his lunch and prompt him to take his tablets; the teatime one, to prepare his evening meal; and the bedtime ones – often as early as 8.30 – to get him sorted for night-time. And there was the one who did the shopping, and the occasional visitor from the church. They were good company, cheery and positive, and he enjoyed the chat. John was a fairly contented kind of guy – apart from missing Jean and this 'damned Arthur-itis …'

John's birthday was coming up soon. It was always noted by his carers and he enjoyed the cards they bought and the silly cakes they baked. He remembered his 70th. 'Too much fuss and bother,' he recalled, though he was genuinely pleased that the big Seven-O hadn't gone past unnoticed.

One Friday his lunchtime carer remarked, 'Birthday coming up soon, John.' 'Aye, right enough,' John replied. 'Seventh of February, eh?' 'Aye, same as last year, and the year before that. It's a remarkable thing, you know, my birthday's been on the seventh of February for as long as

I can remember. It must be some kind of record.' They both laughed.

'It's going to be some kind of record this year, that's for sure,' the carer continued when the laughter had subsided. 'How d'you reckon that?' John asked, intrigued. 'Well,' she went on, 'you're to be seventy-two, right?' 'Aye ...' 'And it's on the seventh of February, isn't it?' 'Aaayyyye,' said John, slowly, trying to grasp the significance of all of this. 'Well, don't you see? That makes you seventy-two on seven/two – seventy-two ... And, on top of all of that, you live at number 72 as well. Seventy-twos all round. Now, that must be *some* kind of record, don't you think?'

John grinned from ear to ear. 'Well, bugger me! 72, on 7/2-72, and living at 72 as well! Blow me down! Would you believe it? ...' 'You should have a party and invite seventy-two people,' the carer suggested. 'Seventy-two people?' John responded, incredulously. 'I don't *know* seventy-two people, far less invite them to a party – if I was inclined to have one anyway ... I doubt if I could have rustled up seventy-two people at *any* time of my life. Seventy-two people? Now, that's a laugh.' The carer left it at that, and carried on with John's lunch. But she had a thought ... *'Seventy-two people? Mmmm ...'*

The morning of John's birthday his morning carers arrived as usual. The post had been and they brought in John's mail, and he was delighted to receive two cards to mark his birthday – one from the church, and one from his carers, and every one of them had signed it and written their own message. The morning carers had brought a bunch of flowers and a box of chocolates – 'From all of us,' they said. John was chuffed. During the morning he had a couple of chocs, admired his birthday cards, and enjoyed the sweet smell of his cut flowers which his carers had arranged in a vase on his mantelpiece.

His lunchtime carer arrived as usual. She seemed very perky, and John remarked on this a couple of times. 'Oh, I enjoy birthdays,' was all she would say. She'd just put John's sandwiches down on his table when the doorbell rang. 'Now, who could that be?' John muttered. 'Let's go and see,' the carer suggested. 'What, both of us?' enquired

John. 'Yes, let's both go.' 'What's going on?' John enquired suspiciously.
Carer and cared-for made their way slowly to the front door. A
chain was removed. A mortise-key was turned. A bolt was drawn. And
a door was slowly opened – to reveal a great crowd of people outside
number 72 Laburnum Avenue. When they saw John in the doorway,
they let out a great cheer, and held up a huge banner which proclaimed in bold, red lettering: '72 people to wish John a very happy
72nd birthday.'

John didn't bother counting. He believed the banner. And when
he felt his carer's arm go around his shoulder as the great crowd sang
'Happy Birthday', he turned to her and said, 'This is your doing, isn't
it?' 'How did you guess?' she whispered. 'If you couldn't rustle up seventy-two people, I reckoned I could. And it's been worth it just to see
your face.'

'Are they all comin' in for a party?' John asked with a worried
frown. 'No, they've got their own arrangements. They'll be off now.
Wave them goodbye.' So John did as he was bid, with a croaky and
tearful 'Thank-you', and an Arthur-itic wave. The crowd dispersed, and
John returned to his birthday-sandwich lunch. 'Seventy-two, seventy-
two ...' was all he could say. 'Seventy-two, now there's a thing ...'

Numbers

Numbers ...
What does it matter how many?

Seventy-six trombones are fine –
a great loud noise no doubt!
But wouldn't one or two melodious-sounding trombones
be equally worthy of our admiration?

A hundred and one dalmatians
make for a great story.

But wouldn't eighty-one, or thirty-seven, or fourteen
be more than enough to be going on with?

Four and twenty blackbirds –
some pie that, don't you think?
But couldn't a few have been spared their demise
to make a sufficient pie-filling for me?

Seventy-two disciples, so we're told,
sent out to do their stuff.
Excellent!
But maybe force of numbers isn't as important
as real commitment from people like me,
and you,
and a few others –
don't you think?

Numbers …
What does it matter how many?

Fourteenth Sunday

Old Testament: 2 Kings 5:1-14
Epistle: Galatians 6:1-16
Gospel: Luke 10:1-11, 16-20

42 Two doughnuts, please

Snax@Mac's was the only café in the High Street. There was a 'Starbucks' at the beginning of the shopping arcade and a 'Costa' in the big bookshop on the square. But *Snax@Mac's* was the only *proper* café in the centre of the town.

Donald MacDonald, the 'Mac' of the name, was proud of his establishment. He'd bought it a couple of years ago and had worked hard to transform it from the 'greasy spoon' kind of place that did little to attract and keep good custom, to the well run, warm and welcoming place it was today.

Snax@Mac's was always busy, especially around lunchtime, and, as the genial and engaging host, Mac knew his regulars well. There were Andy, Chic and Frank, the lads from the tyre-and-exhaust garage a few doors down, with their banter, two filled rolls each, and their mugs of strong 'builder's brew'; there were the Mitchells and the Patersons, two elderly couples who met up at lunchtime without fail, who would scour the menu animatedly, but always order steak pie and chips all round; there were Karen and Louise, shop assistants from the newsagent's across the road, two cheeseburgers (one with onions and one without), two cans of fizzy, and a half-hour of texting and giggles.

Mac had gleaned a fair bit of information about his regulars over the months – Andy from the garage was engaged; Chic fancied Andy's sister; Frank supported United and his two mates didn't; Helen Mitchell was Janice Paterson's sister; Len Mitchell had only one leg; Karen fancied the newsagent's deputy manager, and so did Louise, though Karen reckoned Louise fancied anyone in trousers and that if she played her cards right she could even fix her up with Mac. And so it went on, Mac and his regulars, *Snax@Mac's* doing its job.

Then there was Greig. Mac knew nothing about Greig, apart

from the fact that he was in *Snax@Mac's* every day right on 11.30 –
one cup of black coffee and two jam doughnuts – one in a bag to be
taken away, the other consumed with the coffee at the table by the
window – ten minutes, and no more than a hello, the placing of the
order, a thank you, and a cursory goodbye. Greig had been a regular
for eighteen months or more, and Mac knew as much about Greig
now as he did when he first came in to the café – nothing whatsoever, apart from, that is … every day right on 11.30, one cup of black
coffee, two jam doughnuts, one in a bag, etc, etc.

Not that Mac lost any sleep pondering what insider information
he could glean from or about the taciturn Greig. (He'd only found
out his name because he'd overheard Karen tell Louise she fancied
him and Louise said she knew his name, and it took *ages* for Karen to
get it out of her, and when she did, everyone in the café at the time
got to know …). Mac had more than enough to think about, keeping
Snax@Mac's up to standard and making sure his regular and casual
customers were happy with the only proper café in the High Street.
But he couldn't help wondering occasionally, when Greig was
exiting the café after his brief sojourn, what made this man tick, what
he did for a living, why the regularity of his visits and their timing,
and – just a passing thought – why the second jam doughnut?

All was revealed by chance one Wednesday morning. Mac was late
because he'd had a dental appointment on the other side of town. A
nuisance, but a necessity, and as a result Mac had made arrangements
for the café to be covered by his wife, Penny, and her friend – able and
willing stand-ins. Mac had parked his car in the square and was
walking down to the café not long after 11.30. Well, it must have
been *exactly* 11.40, for there was Greig exiting *Snax@Mac's* right on
time, clutching the familiar white paper bag which Mac knew held
the second of two jam doughnuts. And he was intrigued to see Greig
duck up the alley-way next to the garage and return a minute or so
later – without the bag with the doughnut. Interesting, *very* interesting thought Mac.

186 A blessing to follow

When Greig came into *Snax@Mac's* the next day right on 11.30
- one cup of black coffee, two doughnuts, one in a bag, etc, etc - Mac
wondered if he should ask. He decided not to. But he didn't stop
being intrigued.

So, on the Friday, he asked Penny and her friend to look after the
café for an hour between 11 and 12, and stood at the edge of the
square – and watched. Bang on 11.30 he saw Greig slip into the café,
right on time. At 11.40, he saw him come out clutching the familiar
white paper bag. And he watched him duck up the alley-way next to
the garage and return a minute or so later – without the bag with the
second doughnut.

As Grieg walked off up the High Street, Mac slipped up the
alley-way, and half way up he found the reason for Greig's detour –
for there, sitting on the ground beside the bins at the back door of
the tyre-and-exhaust centre, was an old down-and-out carefully
savouring the last remnants of a jam doughnut.

Remind me

When I get cynical and lose my faith in goodness,
Remind me there are still people who care,
No matter what.

When I get bitter and turn in on myself,
Remind me there are still people who turn outwards to others,
No matter what.

When I get selfish and no one matters but me,
Remind me there are still people who put others first,
No matter what.

When I get too busy and fail to look around me,
Remind me that there are still people who have time to love,
No matter what.

When I get weary with well-doing and give up trying,
Remind me that there are still people who never stop,
No matter what.

Fifteenth Sunday

Old Testament: Amos 7:7-17
Epistle: Colossians 1:1-14
Gospel: Luke 10:25-37

43 Listening

Danny was very different from his brother. For one thing, there were six years between them; for another, Danny was dark-haired like his mother, while his brother took his ginger hair from his dad; but mostly Danny and his brother were different because of what their grandad described as their 'activity levels'. Simply put, Danny was a bit of a couch potato, while, Declan, his younger sibling, was all action.

Declan, aged eight and going on eighteen, was into everything that needed energy. He was captain of the under-nines football team in his school; he attended a gymnastics club on a Monday night and Te Kwan Do on a Wednesday after school; he had his Boys' Brigade night on a Friday, with his marching and PE and games; and in between times he was out with his mates playing football on the Rec, or cycling on the 'cyclo-cross' track the local kids had constructed on the waste ground.

Danny was very different from his brother. It's not that he didn't *like* sport - he enjoyed a kick-about with the best of them and cycled to school every day – it's just that he wasn't into it all of the time. In fact, his ideal evening was to spend time with a good book – not something you could say for many of his peers, far less his little brother – or to go to visit his grandfather.

Danny and Declan's grandfather was an old man. He hailed from Kerry in the south west of Ireland, and, so the boys had learned at an early age, the old man had left his native Ireland after the Second World War and settled and married in the village Danny and Declan had been brought up in. Life had been hard then, especially in the austerity of the post-war years, but a family had been brought up, grandchildren had come along, and the loss of a wife and failing health had been coped with in recent times.

Danny knew all this because of the times he'd spent with his grandad. Indeed, he knew all this and much more besides. He knew what it was like back in Ireland before the war; he'd heard tales of the old man's war service in the heat of the North African desert; he'd listened with fascination to fables and stories, myths and legends from old Celtic culture – or so the old man said, though Danny was sure there were a few made-up stories in there as well; he'd been riveted with accounts of books his grandad had read, and the characters and events and places they contained.

Danny was very different from his brother – for if it was rare for Declan to sit down at all, it was even rarer that he would sit down and listen to his grandad. 'You should come with me sometime when I go to grandad's,' Danny would suggest. 'No, no time to listen to boring old stories …' Declan would reply, as he buzzed off to yet another activity like a miniature version of Billy Whizz. So Danny would listen to his grandad on his own, as another evening of tale-telling unfolded. Sometimes Danny would prompt his grandad to open up new areas of story-telling. 'What was it like being in school back in Kerry, grandad?' he would ask, as the forerunner to more tales of youthful days in Ireland. Sometimes he would encourage the old man to retell a familiar tale, which, like an old friend, Danny was more than happy to meet once again. 'Tell me what happened when you stole the chickens outside Cairo and cooked them on a fire by your tank, grandad …' and an old story would be brought to life again in all its colour and vibrancy.

Danny was very different from his brother. But when their grandad got sick and went to hospital, the two boys were exactly the same. They were worried. Their parents were worried. They all visited the old man in hospital. They knew he was failing. He never recovered. He died in his sleep at the ripe old age of ninety-two. Declan and Danny cried at the funeral. It was that kind of occasion and they were that kind of family. Danny cried more on his own than he ever admitted to anyone. He suspected Declan did the same.

Some weeks after the funeral, Danny made a decision. Grandad may have been dead, but his stories certainly weren't. But they might be if Danny didn't do something about it. So he set himself the task of writing down his grandad's stories. Night after night, with exercise book after exercise book, he'd recall the tales, write them down as he remembered them, and, as he did so, spend time again with his grandad. He'd laugh as he recorded the story of the stolen chickens; he'd cry when he wrote the story of the princess and the wicked witch; he'd work hard to remember the detail of the youthful tales of school. But all the time memories of grandad were being kept alive.

One night, Declan came into Danny's room when he was writing in his exercise book. 'What're you up to bro?' he enquired. 'Have a look,' Danny responded, handing his brother one of the earlier, completed volumes. Declan thumbed through the pages. 'Wow!' he exclaimed. 'Where'd all *this* come from?' 'From grandad,' Danny replied. 'Wow!' Declan repeated. 'Is this all true?' 'Course it is, and all from grandad.'

Danny is still very different from his brother. He has all the stories from grandad and writes them all down. But now Declan comes into his room from time to time – in between bouts of frenetic activity, of course – and sits down, and asks Danny to read him a tale, just as grandad would have told it.

Listen

To listen, and not to speak.

To hear, and not to interrupt.

To pay attention, and not need to respond.

To take note, and not write anything down.

To concentrate, and not miss what's important.

To be silent, and not cut a story short.

To accept, and not try to clarify.
To wait, and not be tired of waiting.
To be still, and not expect anything else to matter.
O God, how hard it is,
And yet, how important …

Sixteenth Sunday

Old Testament: Amos 8:1–12
Epistle: Colossians 1:15–23
Gospel: Luke 10:38–42

44 Harold

'Our Father, who art in heaven, Harold be thy name; thy kingdom come, thy will be done ...'

For as long as Sammy could recall, God was called Harold. After all, he'd say his prayers every Sunday and 'Harold' was right there at the start. Other people called God Harold too when they all said their prayers together in church. He could hear them round about him – 'Harold be thy name ...' So, as far as Sammy was concerned, God's name was Harold. There was no doubt about it.

Sammy and Harold were good mates. It took a fair while for Sammy to figure out that Harold was invisible. He didn't *want* him to be, because he wanted to know just what Harold was like. But he'd come to accept the truth of it – God was invisible. He was always there, though, of that much he was certain. He knew all that Sammy was up to, so Sammy had to be very careful not to do bad things, or at least not *very* bad things. He knew that Harold was a loving God, so he would understand that a little boy couldn't be perfect *all* the time. But he wasn't about to risk making Harold angry by being *really* bad. So, most of the time Sammy did pretty well and stayed fairly good. Sammy and Harold got along just fine.

From time to time, though, Sammy would get to wondering again what Harold was like. He knew he was really old – after all, he'd made the whole world. And he knew he was big and strong – his songs in Sunday School told him that ... and Harold was very, very loving.

Sammy felt safe when he thought about Harold. Even when he had funny feelings in the dark and worried about what might be lurking in the shadows of his bedroom ... and even when he was very, very sad when his pet goldfish died, and his dad had flushed it down the loo before Sammy came home from school so he never had a chance to say goodbye, and he'd cried, and cried, and cried ...

Harold was there, watching over him, keeping him safe. Yes, Sammy and Harold were best mates, and they got along just fine.

So ... Sammy was *extremely* surprised when he heard his mum say that Harold was moving in next door. Harold? Next door? God, moving into number 7? Maybe he'd misheard. He knew that *someone* was moving in next door. He'd seen a massive furniture van pulling up outside when he was on his way to school. So could it be true like his mum said? Was God really moving in next door?

Sammy hovered about the kitchen to overhear his mum chatting with Mrs Valentine from number 3. And it was right enough, 'Harold and Janice,' his mum had said. Harold! HAROLD! Sammy couldn't contain his excitement. He couldn't *wait* to meet with God and see what he was really like. So, when he had watched the big van drive away after teatime, he decided to play round by the side of the house to see if he could catch a glimpse of God.

Imagine his surprise when the front door of number 7 opened and two people – not unlike his mum and dad or even Mrs Valentine from number 3 – emerged carrying mugs of tea, and sat down on the doorstep to survey the scene. 'Perhaps Harold's still inside and these are his bodyguards,' Sammy thought. He wandered casually into the garden of number 7. 'Hello,' he offered. The two folk on the doorstep turned and smiled. 'Hello,' they said in chorus. 'I'm Sammy. I live over there,' said Sammy, turning round and pointing firmly to his own front door. 'Hello, Sammy,' said the lady. 'I'm Janice. Pleased to meet you.' Sammy smiled, and looked over at the man. He smiled back. 'I'm Harold,' he revealed.

Sammy was speechless. His mouth opened wider and wider. His eyes were like saucers. The couple on the doorstep looked at one another, obviously puzzled by the kid's reaction. No one spoke for ages, as Sammy just stared and stared and stared. 'You OK?' Harold asked. 'Are you really God?' Sammy blurted out. Harold threw his head back and guffawed loudly. Janice put her arm round his shoulder. 'That's classic!' she chortled. 'This man? God? Now that's really rich ...'

But Harold seemed to understand that there was something going on here that was more than just an inquisitive kid asking a silly question. He smiled sympathetically. 'What makes you ask that?' he enquired. Sammy could barely raise his voice above a whisper. 'Because God's called Harold ... and you're Harold ... and you've moved in next door ... and I wanted to know what God is like ... and so ...' He'd dried up. There was nothing more he could say.

His new neighbour beamed from ear to ear. 'No, I'm not God,' he said. 'I'm just another Harold.' 'Are you *like* God?' Sammy whispered. 'I suppose I am,' Harold replied, 'just like you are, and just like Janice here. We're all kind of like God, whether we're called Harold, or Janice, or Sammy.' That was enough for Sammy, and he turned slowly and headed back home. Harold and Janice smiled at one another. Janice shrugged her shoulders. 'What was *that* all about?'

The next Sunday in church, Sammy got stuck at the beginning of his prayers. 'Our Father, who art in heaven, Harold be thy name ...' 'Our Father, who art in heaven, Janice be thy name ...' No, it just didn't sound right. 'Our Father, who art in heaven, Sammy be thy name ...' Wow! That sounded strange ... And there and then Sammy decided that he had a lot more thinking to do about God, and he and Harold were going to have a long, *long* chat very soon.

What are you like?

What are you like, God?
Are you like a sunset,
Where purple goes with orange
When they never seemed to match before?

What are you like, God?
Are you a Mozart symphony,
Where goose-bumps happen,
And you want the tingle to last for ever?

What are you like, God?
Are you like the Grand Canyon,
Where silent gasps are the only response,
And even photographs can't capture the wonder?

What are you like, God?
Are you like good sex,
When violins play and choirs sing,
And love blots out everything else?

What are you like, God?
Are you the smile of a child,
Breaking into a bad day,
And making the whole world feel good again?

What are you like, God?
Are you like old Gracie,
Goodness personified
And then multiplied a trillion times over?

What are you like, God?
Are you in the best of worship,
Where praise and prayer are on another level;
When mystery matters more than meaning?

What am I like, God,
Asking all these questions,
When I know I limit you even with the best of my best thoughts
And you're all of these and more?

Seventeenth Sunday

Old Testament: Hosea 1:2-10
Epistle: Colossians 2:6-19
Gospel: Luke 11:1-13

45 A prize possession

Sheila's prize possession was her mother's wedding china. When her mother had moved into a nursing home and the house had to be broken up, Sheila had inherited the half tea-set, and her mother had insisted that it be looked after carefully as it was *very* precious.

To Sheila's knowledge the china had never been used. A cup, saucer and side-plate of the patterned china had been proudly on show in the family display cabinet for as long as she could remember. As far as she was aware that was all there was. But when the attic was being cleared before her mother's move, the remainder of the tea-set was unearthed - five more cups, saucers and side-plates, a milk jug, a sugar bowl and a large plate for cakes, all wrapped in tissue-paper and, it appeared, in its original box.

This had all been confirmed by Sheila's mother as the story of the wedding china was talked through. It had been a gift from her mother and father's bridesmaid for their wedding in 1946, just after the war. It wasn't expensive and wouldn't fetch much even now in any of the TV antique programmes. But it had been the family's symbol of status, and in the cup, saucer and plate with their delicate rose pattern in the display cabinet for all those years – along with father's war medals, the whisky glasses only used at Christmas, and other special artefacts - there had been a symbol of stability, style and status for a family setting up home in the 1950s.

'Why didn't you use it rather than keeping most of it in a box in the attic?' Sheila enquired of her mother. Her mother looked aghast. 'Use it?' she responded. 'Wedding china wasn't for *using*, dear. It would just get spoiled or broken, and that would be just terrible. No, no … The wedding china was too special to be used for 'ordinary', dear, too, too special.'

So the wedding china had become Sheila's prize possession – a cup, saucer and side-plate on show in one of the glass-fronted cupboards in her kitchen; and the rest − in its tissue-paper and original box - lying undisturbed in the cupboard under the stairs.

Mrs Williamson was no different. She was on Sheila's list for pastoral visiting for the church, and Sheila liked Mrs Williamson a lot. She reminded her of her mother, and so Sheila and this housebound elderly lady had become good friends. And Mrs Williamson had a cup, saucer and side-plate on show in her ancient display cabinet in the corner of her living room.

Sheila remarked on the items in the cabinet one day. 'Oh,' Mrs Williamson replied with pride, 'that's my grandmother's wedding china, or at least part of it. She was married in 1870, and the wedding china was a gift from her parents. It's a full tea-set. Victorian, "Limoges", you know, and probably worth a lot of money.' 'So where's the rest, Mrs Williamson?' Sheila enquired. 'Oh it's carefully wrapped in boxes in the cupboard in the back room,' Mrs Williamson responded, her voice dropping to a whisper, in case anyone should overhear the whereabouts of her secret stash of expensive china. 'It's never been touched. Too precious for that; handed down from my grandmother to my mother, and from my mother to me; the family's prize possession.' 'Never been used, not ever, not even on special occasions?' Sheila continued. 'Goodness no! That would make it ordinary, and then it wouldn't be special, would it?'

Some time later, Sheila was distressed to hear that Mrs Williamson's house had been broken into not long after the old lady had been taken off to hospital with a suspected stroke. Thankfully, not much had been stolen as the thieves had been disturbed … but not before they had made a right mess of the house − papers pulled from drawers, cupboards ransacked, and ornaments smashed to smithereens.

Sheila got a team together from the church to help clean up the house. 'Such a shame,' said one of the work-party. 'It's just as well Mrs Williamson doesn't know,' said another. And they set to work to bring the house back to some semblance of order. But it was when they went into the back room that everyone realised that it would be impossible to restore Mrs Williamson's home to its pristine condition. For the contents of the corner cupboard had been strewn over the floor, the cardboard boxes tipped upside down scattering their contents everywhere. And all over the place they could clearly see the shattered remains of a Victorian Limoges tea-set, Mrs Williamson's prize possession, smashed into a thousand pieces.

Sheila and her friends stood in the midst of the chaos and wept, such was the devastation and their grief for Mrs Williamson and her precious tea-set, her grandmother's unused wedding china.

Later that evening when Sheila got home she delved into her cupboard under the stairs and unearthed the major part of the half tea-set that had been her mother's wedding china. Laying it out on the kitchen table, she added to it the cup, saucer and side-plate that had been on display in the glass-fronted cupboard, and stood back to admire the six cups, saucers and side-plates, the milk jug and sugar bowl, and the large plate for cakes, all with their delicate rose pattern. Sheila smiled and announced out loud, 'Well mother, you may not like this, but I've made a decision today – *this* tea-set, our prize possession, is now going to be used for "ordinary".'

Stuff

My Granny used to say,
'You come into the world with nothing,
and you'll go out with nothing.'

I never knew – or allowed myself to know –
what that meant.
For, after all,
hadn't I accumulated lots of stuff
over the years,
and didn't that stuff belong to me?

Stuff around me that I couldn't do without …
Stuff in my cupboards that I'll get around to sorting some day …
Stuff in my garage that I can't bear to throw out …
Stuff that I'd hate to lose if my house went on fire …
Stuff that's insured because it's worth a lot …
Stuff that's uninsurable but has great sentimental value …
Stuff that moves with me when I change houses …
Stuff that's mine …
Stuff that belongs to no one but me …

And God says, 'You fool!'
(And I suspect that's what my Granny would have said too,
because, even if you *think* it's your stuff,
you can't take it with you when you go.)

'You come into the world with nothing …'
and even though you've picked up lots of stuff along the way,
it was only ever on loan; and so,
'You'll go out with nothing',
nothing whatsoever.'

Stuff …
What's it matter?
Fool that you are …

Eighteenth Sunday

Old Testament: Hosea 11:1-11
Epistle: Colossians 3:1-11
Gospel: Luke 12:13-21

46 The warning

The burglary at 22a Forthspring Close had left Miss Constance McGavigan feeling very shaky indeed. Constance couldn't help wondering if it was the start of a major crime-wave in her quiet cul-de-sac. It had been Alfie, her neighbour across the stair, who had been the unfortunate victim. But living in 22b made Constance feel very vulnerable indeed.

Alfie hadn't lost much in the break-in. He was in the habit of leaving his door open when he popped down to the shops of a morning to buy his paper and breakfast rolls. And one morning the temptation had obviously been too much for an opportunist thief. So when Alfie returned, he was minus his radio from his kitchen and his umbrella and walking stick from the stand by the front door. Not much of a haul for the local criminal fraternity to gloat over. But a burglary is a burglary. And Miss Constance McGavigan didn't like it one little bit.

She was delighted, therefore, when she got a phone call from the local police asking if one of their constables could come and interview her as part of their door-to-door enquiries. An hour or so later, Constance was welcoming WPC Kelly Harrison to her home. 'Nice young lady,' Constance had mused. That's why she thought she'd better give the WPC 'The Warning'! The Warning was given by Constance to all newcomers to her home. Regular callers were well prepared, but WPC Harrison, being new to the McGavigan abode, and being 'a nice young lady', needed The Warning.

'Thank you for coming,' Constance offered, shaking the young police constable by the hand. 'Come away in. But be careful of Dougal. He's not too good with strangers. Better to talk very quietly. That way it'll give him time to get used to you. OK?' 'OK,' replied Kelly, not bothering to enquire who Dougal might be or the nature of his antipathy to strangers. After all, she'd become familiar with the dangers of family homes – from alsatian dogs to violent husbands; from vicious cats to neanderthal teenagers. So, grateful nonetheless for The Warning, WPC Kelly Harrison followed Constance from the hallway into the lounge.

There was no sign of Dougal. Kelly glanced around the room. No growling dog under the sideboard; no aggressive male lurking in the doorway; no suspicious moggy eyeing her from its favourite cushion; no gangly teenager following her into the room.

She was relieved! Perhaps Dougal had slipped out, or gone to the loo, or been locked in a cupboard, or consigned to the garden. In any event, Constance didn't seem too bothered as she sat in the big chair by the fire. And Kelly reckoned she didn't need to worry about The Warning after all. So she took out her notebook. 'Well, Miss McGavigan,' she pronounced boldly, 'I just wanted to ask you a few questions about …'

She never had the chance to finish her sentence. For that's when she realised that The Warning was amply justified. For Dougal was none other than a kamikaze budgie who, as Constance had warned, didn't like strangers one bit. In a yellow and green flash, with a whirring of wings and a high-pitched 'cheep' that was worthy of an ornithological specimen twice his size, Dougal dived down from his perch at the end of the curtain rail and headed straight for the hairdo of the hitherto immaculately groomed WPC Kelly Harrison.

Kelly ducked. Too late! For the recalcitrant Dougal skimmed the side of her head, pulling out much of her hair from its restraining pins, and leaving her auburn locks hanging limply over her right cheek. 'That's Dougal,' Constance offered – as if Kelly hadn't figured that out already. 'He'll be fine if you don't talk too loud, just till he gets used to you.'

'OK, I'll try,' Kelly whispered, trying to regain her composure. Not whispering quietly enough, clearly, for the kamikaze Dougal launched another sortie, this time leaving an unfortunate WPC with even less composure and even more of her hairdo straggling over her forehead. 'Too loud,' Constance suggested. 'OK,' Kelly replied, mouthing the words, her voice barely audible. But not inaudible enough for death-mission Dougal as he swooped down for a third time. And despite Kelly's attempt at evading action, Dougal had now reduced her hairstyle to something that looked like it had been dragged through a hedge backwards.

'Best not speak at all,' Constance said, as the beady-eyed Dougal watched suspiciously from his perch on the candelabra on the sideboard. It was the only interview WPC Kelly Harrison had ever conducted in total silence – at least from her side. She wrote down her questions in her notebook, handed it to Constance, who verbalised her answers. It took twice as long as usual. But they got there in the end – and without any further interruptions from the maniacal Dougal.

In time, Constance was showing the bedraggled but very relieved Kelly out into the hall. Safe now from Dougal the kamikaze budgie, Kelly thanked Constance for her time and suggested there was no need for her to worry. 'Do you think I should get a guard dog or have a burglar alarm fitted, just to keep me safe?' Constance enquired. Kelly smiled, flicked several strands of auburn hair from her face and shook Miss Constance McGavigan by the hand. 'No need,' she replied, reassuringly, 'as long as any would-be burglars aren't struck totally dumb or haven't been given The Warning, I think Dougal is all the protection you'll ever need.'

Careful!

Help me to heed the warning signs …
As I'm careful crossing the street,
help me to be careful crossing from the old to the new;
as I'm careful with Health and Safety,
help me to be careful with the health of my soul

and the safety of my love;
as I'm careful on an icy road,
help me to be careful when I'm sliding into bad habits;
as I'm careful with what I carry,
help me to be careful carrying worries and concerns,
for myself and others;
as I'm careful with my time,
help me to be careful with the things of eternity.

Nineteenth Sunday

Old Testament: Isaiah1:1, 10–20
Epistle: Hebrews 11:1–3, 8–16
Gospel: Luke 12:32–40

47 Division

Gary and Elizabeth always enjoyed their holidays on the islands of Scotland. 'We collect islands,' Gary was happy to remark when he told his work colleagues that he and his wife were off on yet *another* jaunt to explore the remoteness and beauty of Scottish island life. The islands never failed to give them what they needed, and they always returned refreshed and invigorated, with yet another batch of island photographs.

Keen photographers, Gary and Elizabeth enjoyed their attempts to capture the magic of their explorations and would spend many a happy winter evening playing around with their digital photos, cropping this one, touching up the colour of that one, and marvelling at the quality of another. There wasn't a room in their home where the walls or surfaces weren't adorned with a photograph or two from their island holidays.

In recent times, Elizabeth had taken to recording what she called her more 'quirky' images – what Gary often described as her 'arty-farty stuff'. But it gave Elizabeth a lot of pleasure to find pictures that were 'out of the ordinary' and different from the usual touristy views. The crumbling drystane dyke in the rain; the higgledy-piggledy stack of lobster creels in the evening light; the croft-house with its red roof on one side and green roof on the other – all committed to the digital camera, and all to give lasting pleasure and delight.

But no picture intrigued and delighted her more than her photograph of the blue boat that had been cut in half. She'd come across it earlier that year when she and Gary were travelling home to their rented cottage along a remote island road. They turned a corner on a windy, single-track road, and there it was, a few yards from the side of the road, sitting on the top of a raised mound – a blue rowing boat, in two pieces, side by side. 'Stop the car, stop …' she ordered. 'Another photo-opportunity,' Gary murmured, as he pulled the car into the next lay-by.

Soon Elizabeth was being creative with a blue boat in two parts, and Gary had to admit he was mighty intrigued. The boat, in perfect shape, painted a deep blue, was about twelve feet long – or it would have been had it remained in one piece. And the two parts hadn't separated because of rotten wood. The boat had been sawn in half right through the middle! No doubt about it, the blue boat had been split in two – quite deliberately.

It turned out that Elizabeth had taken some good pictures of the blue boat in two pieces – 'Very stylish', Gary had to admit - and they both agreed that the best of the photographs would do well enlarged, printed, framed, and hung in the hall.

That's why the blue boat in two pieces was one of the first things Father James saw when he came to visit Gary and Elizabeth's home. Father James was the new priest in the parish, and, as a courtesy, a few weeks after his arrival, Gary and Elizabeth had invited him round for supper. Imagine their surprise when, stopping in the hallway right in front of Elizabeth's star photograph, Father James exclaimed, 'Good grief. It's Donald McKillop's boat!' Gary and Elizabeth couldn't wait to hear how a city priest could know *anything* about this obscure artefact. And over pre-supper nibbles and a dram, they got the whole story. 'I passed that very boat when I was on holiday there late last year,' he told them, 'and, like you, I couldn't figure out what had happened to such a fine boat to leave it in a state like that. I was staying with the local priest on the island, so, over dinner, I remarked on the strange sight of the blue rowing boat cut in two. "Aye, well, well now, but that'll be Donald McKillop's boat, right enough." "But what's it doing in two pieces on the side of the road?" I enquired of my knowledgeable friend. "O, well, well now," the priest continued, "it was a terrible thing. For old Donald died and left his boat to his two sons for them to share. Well, well, but the two sons never got on and never could they agree who was to get the boat for the fishing one day and who the other, and if they had gone out in the boat together, och, well, only the good Lord knows what they would have done to each other, for one would be rowing one way and one the other, just for spite. It was the talk of the village. One of them was going to hurt the other over the sake of their father's boat. Then, one day, they came to an agreement – the only thing the two sons have agreed on from that day till this – that they would share the boat, right enough, but by cutting the damned thing in two. And that's just what they did. And the whole village turned out to watch - and I was there myself – as the two boys, one on one side and one on the other, with a big band-saw, cut the blue boat in half, and declared themselves satisfied."

'So that's the story of the picture in your hall. It's Donald McKillop's boat, shared out equally between his two sons, a fair division - apart from the fact that the beautiful blue boat never sailed again.'

Gary and Elizabeth take great delight in showing visitors their 'arty-farty' photograph of Donald McKillop's boat and telling the story of its sad demise. But they've lost count of the number of people who've stated the obvious – that it would have been better to work out a more sensible way to share a boat than cutting it in half and leaving it by the side of a remote island road, never to sail again.

Divisions

It's interesting, isn't it, and somewhat disturbing too, to think about the things that divide us rather than draw us together. So, why not take a little time to think about it, and find it interesting for yourself, and be disturbed a little too.

In relationships, with family and friends, what divides us, and what can be done to overcome these divisions?

In church and community, where do divisions get in the way, and what can be done to pull down the barriers?

In society, in our wider world, what are the divisions that separate us from one another, and how do we build bridges?

In faith, what divides us from living fully in God's love, and what difference do we need in our attitude that will remove the divisions?

It's interesting, and challenging, isn't it, when a perfectly good boat can't sail because of the divisions we've created …

Twentieth Sunday

Old Testament: Isaiah 5:1–7
Epistle: Hebrews 11:29–12:2
Gospel: Luke 12:49–56

48 Victoria

There wasn't *supposed* to be a cat in the crematorium … well, not during Auntie May's funeral service anyway. At least that's what the funeral director told the family outside afterwards … It's not that this particular cat wasn't well known around the crematorium grounds. For Victoria – for such was her name – had been around the place for as long as most folk could remember. 'Victoria'? The black coat, white collar and the little, fuzzy white patch on her forehead made this cat's name the obvious choice. And 'She's a great mouser!' the crematorium staff would tell you if you cared to ask.

But there wasn't supposed to be a cat *in* the crematorium during Auntie May's funeral service, or any other service for that matter. How the bold Victoria managed to slip inside, no one knew. But she soon made her presence well enough known to all who were there.

The first person to notice the cat was the vicar. Well, 'notice' isn't quite accurate. 'Feel' would be more appropriate. For having intimated the first lesson, and now a few words into the beginning of the Twenty-third Psalm, 'The Lord is my Shepherd …', she felt an odd sensation on the skin of her right calf. Thinking it might be a sudden draught from the side door, or a stray insect which had alighted on her leg, she casually flicked her other foot across the site of the sensation only to find the gentle movement being responded to with a loud and clearly irritated 'Meow!' followed by a more satisfied 'Purrrr' as Victoria returned to the pleasure of using the vicar's right leg as a sensual rubbing-post.

Seconds later, Victoria decided to reveal herself to the assembled company. She slinked out from under the security of the vicar's cassock and stretched herself to her full length on the top step of the dais, in full view of the startled mourners. There were audible whispers among the congregation. The vicar struggled to maintain her composure, but decided it was best to carry on regardless. So, having rediscovered the place in the reading, on she went. And on went Victoria too, apparently considering it appropriate to continue her explorations of the crematorium's furnishings – no matter what the vicar or anyone else was doing at the same time … 'He maketh me to lie down in green pastures …' and Victoria was walking languidly across the top of the altar; 'Yea though I walk through the valley …' and Victoria had moved on to an investigation of the bass pedals of the crematorium organ; 'Thou prepareth a table before me …' and Victoria was dipping a searching paw into the vicar's water glass; 'Surely goodness and mercy shall follow me …' and Victoria was padding gracefully along the book-rest of the mourners' front pew. And so it continued, the vicar doing her best, but the performing Victoria clearly the star turn!

But it was 'The Committal' of Auntie May's remains that worried the vicar the most, the coffin moving through the final curtains, potentially followed by the ever-adventurous Victoria, with the accompanying risk of an over-inquisitive cat disappearing into the working end of the crematorium – with all nine lives being threatened at once. The vicar needn't have worried though, for Victoria wasn't all that interested in the moving coffin, choosing instead to amuse herself by playing with the tassels on the end of the lectern-Bible's book markers.

When the final hymn had been sung and the blessing pronounced, a relieved vicar and some bemused mourners gathered outside the crematorium to exchange their gratitude and good wishes. But quickly, and not surprisingly, Victoria the unexpected mourner became the topic of conversation.

The vicar felt obliged to offer her apologies for the intrusion of a cat and for the way it had spoiled Auntie May's funeral service, robbing it of the dignity and thoughtfulness it deserved. But for a second time that morning, the vicar needn't have worried. 'No apology needed, vicar,' she was told. 'It was the best part of the service.' 'It was *so* right for Auntie May.' 'She was such a great lover of cats herself, wasn't she right enough?' 'Aye, it was a sign.' 'It couldn't have been better.' 'The cat was OK.' 'Auntie May must have had a hand in this.'

The vicar offered an embarrassed smile, half of bemusement and half of relief, and she resolved there and then that if Victoria interrupted one of her services again, she'd probably leave her to get on with doing her own thing – always assuming that the deceased was a lover of cats, of course.

For Victoria had clearly enabled Auntie May's family and friends to make more sense of a funeral service than had been possible for a jobbing vicar. After all, with her black coat and white collar, it could be said that Victoria was half way to being a vicar already!

Bent double

Crippled ...
Bent over, not able to straighten up,
and for thirty years, for goodness' sake.
Bent double ...

Have you ever been bent double?
You know,
the kind of 'bent double' position
when you try to touch your toes?

Try it, if you're up for it ...
Even if you can't get all the way down –
and I know *I* can't –
bend over as far as you're able.
Got it?

Now stay there for a time.
Be bent double for thirty seconds, never mind thirty years ...

What can you see?
Your feet ...
About a metre arc of floor ...
And not much else ...

Can you see someone smile?
Can you catch a sunset?
Can you take in a beautiful scene?
Can you watch a movie?
Can you offer someone a kiss?
Can you reach up to a shelf?
No?
Because you're bent double, aren't you,
and your world is limited to what's around your feet.

God, come to my Sabbath,
come to my synagogue,
come to my brokenness,
come to my inability to stand up straight,
come to my limited view,
place your hands upon me,
lift me up straight
that I might see again
and give you all my praise.

Twenty-first Sunday

Old Testament: Jeremiah 1:4-10
Epistle: Hebrews 12:18-29
Gospel: Luke 13:10-17

49 Strangers together

It was the first time Bert had visited the village. He'd found it on his favourite tourism website, and that had led him to a B&B over an autumn weekend. He enjoyed this kind of mini-break, exploring a new part of the country, picking up interesting pieces of local history, doing a bit of bird-watching, appreciating his own company, and, of course, going to a new church on the Sunday.

Bert had been to all sorts of churches, all over the place, some good, some bad, some indifferent. But it was always interesting, and he never failed to take something from a new place that helped him on his way – a message, a lesson, an insight, or whatever.

In actual fact, visiting new churches was always an important part of Bert's weekends away, and he regularly took a photograph of a new church and recorded some information about it in his 'Churches' Notebook'. 'I could write a book about the churches I've been to,' Bert told a friend once. 'Maybe you should,' the friend had responded. 'Though I'm not sure it would ever be a best seller.'

Well, best seller or not, Bert was pleased to explore the village church during his current weekend away. The church building wasn't much to look at, and, if he was honest, the service didn't offer much to raise the spirits. He doubted whether it would have merited more than a couple of lines in the embryonic 'Churches I Have Known'. The singing was good, though, and Bert was encouraged by the fact that there were a couple of tunes he was well familiar with. He enjoyed that. It was his message for this weekend. But that was about all.

So, when the service was over, Bert swithered as to whether he should go through to the church halls for the obligatory 'after service coffee' as invited in the church notices. These tended to be hit-and-miss affairs, and, like the church services themselves, there were the good, the bad and the downright ugly. However, encouraged by the aroma of fresh-brewed coffee wafting from the bowels of the building – now, there was something a bit better than most – Bert made his way through to the room where coffee and tea were on offer.

It was all standard stuff, and, having deposited his payment in the money-collecting sugar bowl, he picked up his coffee and plain biscuit and looked for a place to sit. There was plenty of choice. Three elderly ladies didn't seem too keen on a visitor taking the spare place at their table. A couple with a wriggly child looked a bit too risky for Bert's liking. Neither of the two men at the table in the corner appeared interested in inviting him over. It was all standard stuff.

So, as usual, Bert decided not to expect too much and headed for a table by the window occupied by one middle-aged man on his own. Safe choice, Bert thought. Approaching the table he enquired politely, 'Is there anyone sitting here?' (… as you do, even though it was obvious there wasn't!) 'No, help yourself,' the gent replied, beckoning Bert to sit down on a spare chair of his choosing. Bert chose the chair opposite the man.

'How are you?' Bert enquired. 'I'm fine. And you?' 'Not too bad.' 'Nice morning,' the man offered. 'Yes indeed, not too bad at all.' And the two men lapsed into a somewhat uncomfortable silence.

After a time, Bert decided this wasn't good enough. 'I'm a stranger here,' he offered. 'Your first time, then?' the man enquired. 'Yes, the first time,' Bert responded. 'Let me welcome you, then,' suggested the man, and, offering Bert his hand, gave him a firm, welcoming handshake. 'I'm John,' he confirmed, 'good to meet you.'

There was another awkward silence. Bert decided to have another go. 'Are you a stranger too?' Bert asked of his companion. 'Yes, very much so,' John responded. 'First time for you, then?' Bert enquired. 'No,' the man replied, 'I've been coming here for over a year and you're the first person who's bothered to come to say hello.'

Strangers

Are strangers really strange?
Or are they friends we don't yet know?

Do strangers think I'm strange?
Or will they think I'm even stranger when they get to know me?

God, help me with strangers and with strangeness ...
Or is that too strange a prayer to ask?

Twenty-second Sunday

Old Testament: Jeremiah 2:4-13
Epistle: Hebrews 13:1-8, 15-16
Gospel: Luke 14:1, 7-14

50 What lasts?

Sandy always tried to find a labouring job during the long summer breaks from college. For a start, such jobs were usually paid well. But, more importantly, it meant he didn't have to think too much. Thinking was for college. Vacations were for switching off from all of that.

One summer he managed to land his dream job - working with a firm repairing the single-track roads in the north west of Scotland. It was fairly mundane labouring work - good money, lots of fun, the occasional busy day, and lots of wonderful characters to work with. Sandy reckoned he learned more that summer about real life and real people than he ever learned in the ivory towers of Theological College.

On the final week on one remote stretch of Highland road, the foreman called Sandy into the hut. 'You've done well, son,' the gruff but amiable charge-hand began. 'So me and the boys have decided to offer you a bonus. We're putting back the road-signs now this stretch is finished. There's a 'Road Narrows' sign to be put up just before the narrow bridge, and we'd like to give you the honour of doing that. We can't put a plaque up to say it was you. But, in years to come, if you ever drive past this way with your kids, you can tell them, "Your dad did that." It'll be your lasting memorial.'

So, on the Friday afternoon the squad gathered together down by the bridge to witness the erection of what had become known as 'Sandy's Sign'. With the guidance of skilled practitioners, and the graphic, words-of-one-syllable advice from seasoned labourers, the road-sign was soon in place. There was a round of applause. Sandy took a bow. His lasting legacy – 'Sandy's Sign' - was there for all to admire.

Sandy was chuffed to bits, and, like a wee boy with a new toy, he was keen to show people that he had made his mark - a sign by a narrow bridge that proved he'd done his bit. So on the Sunday afternoon he took his mum and dad for a run in the car, up a Highland road, towards a narrow bridge, to marvel at the sign of their son's mark on the world. But when they reached the bridge there was no 'Road Narrows' sign to be seen. Sandy drove on a bit, turned the car in the entrance to a field, and drove across the narrow bridge from the other side. Still no sign to be seen. A turn around again a bit further on and a final drive back to the bridge. No, there was definitely no sign at all.

Sandy parked the car in the next lay-by, told his somewhat bemused parents to wait for a bit, and walked back to the narrow bridge for closer look. He found the sign, right enough. But instead of it standing proudly where he had erected it only two days before, he found it lying forlornly in a muddy ditch. Bent and twisted, it had clearly been demolished by a lorry, or some other large passing vehicle. Sandy was told later he'd put it too close to the road. The sign never had a chance. It hadn't lasted a day.

What lasts?

'What lasts?' we ask, when pondering the worth of what we've done.
What will the world remember when each one is dead and gone?
What impact will remain to show the difference we've made?
And will we be remembered as the ones who've made the grade?

Will generations yet to come recall what we've achieved?
Might they rejoice and marvel at the tapestry we've weaved?
Can signs remain for ever showing we've been past this way?
Will changes we have made outlive the passing of our day?

Will what we thought was special be remembered by the rest?
Might we be singled out for praise reserved for just the best?
Will what we have accomplished mean a plaque can mark our fame?
Will people talk of eminence when mentioning our name?

O child, you'll be remembered not by things that will not last,
Like merit, style or prominence, or kudos, rank or class,
Or accolades that make you seem august and grandiose,
But by your help for others who have needed you the most.

Where love has changed a life, then you'll be worthy of our praise;
Where brokenness found healing, then a voice in thanks we'll raise;
When poverty was challenged, then you'll be recalled with pride;
If justice was your watchword, then your worth can't be denied.

The things of time will soon decay and crumble into dust;
For transience can never offer substance we can trust;
If you want immortality, kiss the things of time goodbye,
And grasp what is eternal – then your love will never die.

Twenty-third Sunday

Old Testament: Jeremiah 18:1-11
Epistle: Philemon 1-21
Gospel: Luke 14:25-33

51 Lost and found

Benny's grandfather had been a sailor. 'During the war …' he would tell Benny at the beginning of another of his long stories about big ships, and Atlantic convoys, and stormy seas, and much more besides. It sounded like such an adventurous life – although Benny learned later that his grandfather only told him the parts he felt he should hear, and never, ever touched on the danger and the fear from 'During the war …'

Benny's grandfather had still been a sailor after the war too. He'd crewed on a little fishing-boat from the harbour in the next village. There weren't so many stories about that, Benny discovered, but that was OK. His grandfather's tales from 'During the war' were more than enough.

Because Benny's grandfather had been a sailor he knew a lot about boats. That knowledge, however, didn't translate into the model-boat-building that other old sailors in the seaside villages were famous for. Scale models of fishing boats from down the years adorned most of the windows in the streets round the harbours. But none of them had been made by Benny's grandfather. That just wasn't his thing. Stories? Great. Skill with his hands? No chance.

That's why Benny was apprehensive when he got a sailing-boat kit for his birthday when he was ten years old. It seemed too compli-cated for him to do on his own, and his father had even less skill with his hands than his grandfather. However, Benny's grandfather wasn't going to see the young lad stuck, so the two of them, old man and young boy, had a go. It took them ages. Sometimes they made mis-takes. Sometimes they had a real laugh together when disasters hap-pened. Sometimes they just abandoned it for the time being, organised some juice and biscuits, and grandfather would tell some more stories. But eventually the little sail-boat was done, and with sails and rigging and a little Saltire flag on the top of the mast – 'It's a Scottish boat, after all,' grandfather had said – it was ready for trying out on the pond in the park.

The only thing that was missing was a name. 'Let's call it "Atlantic Convoy",' Benny suggested. Grandfather seemed more than happy with that, and so, in his very best writing, Benny wrote "Atlantic Convoy" in red felt-tip pen along the side, and they were ready to go!

Benny enjoyed the times when he and his grandfather played with *Atlantic Convoy* on the pond in the park. Sometimes, when the wind was right, the boat would scoot across the pond perfectly. Other times, it would just sit there at the edge with not a lot happening. But it was always fun, more because of time with grandfather than with the boat, because it was their boat.

Benny was twenty-two when his grandfather died. The old man had become really frail, and sailing *Atlantic Convoy* on the pond in the park had been discontinued long since. But Benny still had his stories, and, more importantly, he still had his boat. They were his connection with his grandfather, and, as such, they were very, very important.

He knows *now* that it was really silly to take the little boat down to the shore and sail it in the sea. All he was trying to do was to remember his grandfather, and taking *Atlantic Convoy* to sail at the edge of the big sea seemed to be the right thing to do. But it wasn't. A sudden gust of wind and a pulling tide had taken the little boat far beyond the shore. Benny waded in as far as he could. But it was too late. *Atlantic Convoy* had gone, taken away from him by the cruel sea. No one will know how much Benny cried that day. It was as if he'd lost his last tangible link to his grandfather.

Life moved on, and Benny came to terms with his loss. Marriage and the arrival of twin boys gave much meaning to his life. He regretted the loss of his grandfather's boat, of course, but he still had the stories, and he was *so* keen to tell his kids some of the stories he'd learned as a young boy and keep his grandfather alive for his own sons.

Imagine his surprise, therefore, when, in a junk-shop in a town where he was on business, he saw a little sail-boat in the window. He did a double take. He stared at it for ages. Yes, it was unmistakable. It was *Atlantic Convoy*. The sail was torn. The name was smudged. But it was his and his grandfather's boat for sure. Breathless, he rushed into the shop. 'That's my boat!' he said to a startled owner. 'No way!' was the sullen response. 'I bought that boat fair and square. Piece of junk it may be. But it's mine to sell, not yours to claim.' 'How much is it selling for, then?' Benny continued. 'Twenty-five quid,' the owner suggested. 'Twenty-five quid?' Benny stuttered. The sullen junk-shop owner seemed to take this as the start of a haggling process, and shot back, 'Ok, twenty quid'll do.' 'Done!' offered Benny, knowing full well he would have paid *much* more to retrieve his precious memento. So, a crisp twenty pound note was exchanged for a little sail-boat roughly wrapped in newspaper and stuffed into a blue plastic bag.

When Benny got home with *Atlantic Convoy* he smiled and cried at the same time as he unwrapped his valuable purchase. It took him a week or so to restore it to its original condition. Now it sits on a high shelf in the twins' bedroom ready for the day when it can be the prompt for telling the stories an old sailor had told him, and maybe even to play with on the pond in the village with two excited little boys. *Atlantic Convoy*, made and enjoyed, lost and found, welcomed back and cherished for ever, and always, *always* loved.

Redeemed

I made you, God said.
I know, said I.
I lost you, God said.
I'm sorry, said I.
I found you, God said.

I'm grateful, said I.

I redeemed you, God said.

I'm amazed, said I.

I love you, God said.

I know, said I.

Twenty-fourth Sunday

Old Testament: Jeremiah 4:11-12, 22-28

Epistle: 1 Timothy 1:12-17

Gospel: Luke 15:1-10

52 The brown coat

Jim always kept a brown coat hanging in the cupboard of his office. It was an old brown coat and it had belonged to his father. Jim's father had been a storeman in the rubber mill down by the canal. The brown coat had been his uniform for many years, and, by the looks of it, the coat hadn't been replaced over those many years either. The right-hand pocket had been stitched; there was a patch just below the waist at the back; there was an oil stain on the cuff of the left sleeve. But it had been his father's working coat, and it was one of Jim's most cherished possessions.

'The first in the family to go to university!' Jim was proud of that label, but nowhere near as proud as his dad had been when he had attended Jim's graduation. When he was little, his dad had asked him, 'What do you want to be when you grow up, son?' 'I want to wear a brown coat and be a storeman like you, daddy,' Jim had replied. He would remember to his dying day the look of horror on his father's face and the words of the stern reply: 'You'll do better than that, lad. I had to leave school when I was 14. Money was tight. There were nippers in the family below me to be fed. I never had the chance of a good education. But you ... You can do better, lad. You can do better.' And he had ...

A first class honours degree and an MBA to follow had given Jim the chance his father never had. And now, aged thirty-seven, he was financial controller of one of the largest engineering factories in the expanding industrial estate which stood on the site of the long-since demolished rubber factory down by the canal. A sharp suit and black, polished shoes; a fancy office with a big desk; impressive diplomas on the wall; a very responsible job ... Yes, indeed, Jim *had* done better, and his dad would have been very, very proud.

Jim's father would have been even *more* proud if he'd known what

Jim got up to once every week. For, usually on a Friday afternoon, Jim would don the old, brown, storeman's coat, slip down the back stair, and take a walk through the factory floor, usually ending up in the storeroom in one of the factory's production sections. He got to know the men. He canvassed their views on things. He joined in the banter about football and politics.

As far as they were concerned, he was Jimmy, from one of the other storerooms in one of the other production areas. As far as Jim was concerned, it was one of the most important times of the week, and it was one of the things that informed Jim's thinking when the management board had their Monday morning meetings, and especially when they got on to talk about workforce morale and job conditions. Jim knew about these things – or at least Jimmy the storeman did!

One Friday afternoon, Jim found himself in the houf* in one corner of the factory. Two of the lads were on a tea-break when Jim joined them. 'Hiya, Jimmy. Fancy a brew?' Bobby, the younger of the two, enquired. And before any response was offered, Jim had a steaming mug of tea in his hand. 'Tam's toilin', so he is,' the tea-maker said, 'aren't you, son?' Tam nodded silently 'His maw's died, ken? Ah wis tellin' you she was poorly, eh? Well, she slipped away on Wednesday, eh, Tam?' Tam nodded again. 'I'm sorry for your loss, Tam,' Jim offered. 'An' as if that wisnae bad enough,' the tea-maker commentator continued, 'there's the funeral tae sort, an' money's tight, eh, Tam?' Tam nodded once more, and all three men lapsed into an awkward silence.

In time, his brew finished and final words of sympathy offered, Jim took his leave. He was back in the houf at lunchtime the following Monday. Bobby was on his own, wolfing down a doorstep cheese-and-pickle sandwich and draining a huge mug of tea. 'Hiya, Jimmy. This is no' Friday, eh? Whit brings you here the day?' 'Tam's not in, is

---

* A houf is a workperson's rest area.

he?' Jim enquired. 'Naw. Funeral's on Thursday, so he's off for the week.' 'Will you see him before the funeral?' asked Jim. 'Aye. Ah'm going' roon after work the day tae see how he is, ken?' 'Good,' Jim continued. 'When you're there, will you give him this?' and, with that, he handed Bobby a large buff envelope. 'Some of the lads have had a whip round. There's some readies in there to help with the funeral.'

Jim took the Thursday afternoon off to attend Tam's mum's funeral. He sat at the back, slipping away quietly at the end without speaking to anyone. When Tam got back to work a couple of weeks later, Bobby told him he'd heard that one of the managers had been at the funeral, but he didn't know which one. 'Did you see him?' Tam asked. 'Naw, an' how would ah know any of the managers, ken? No bloody manager ever ventures doon here. Stuck in their fancy offices, nae clue aboot the likes o' us, ken?' 'Well, I'm sure wan o' them was there, at the back, flash suit and fancy haircut, that poncy guy who fiddles a' the money stuff. Ah'm *sure* ah saw him, eh? An' d'you know somethin'? He's a dead ringer for yon Jimmy the storeman who organised yon' whip-round, ken?' 'Jimmy? Aye, he's some guy, eh? There's no' a manager who's a patch on Jimmy the storeman, ken?'

Back in his office, Jim was taking his brown coat out of his cupboard and was thinking about which of the factory's storerooms he was going to visit today …

Goodness

It's not your social standing that's the meaning you still seek.
It's what you choose to stand up for that makes your life unique.
It's not what you'll be known for now
that makes more eyebrows raise –
But what you show of goodness all your days.

It's not how you're rewarded by the trappings of success,
But what rewards you offer those whose lives you're called to bless.
It's not enough that people sing your name in hymns of praise –
It's what you show of goodness all your days.

It's not the riches of the world that make your treasure store,
But what enriches those who know your love, and need still more.
It's not how you present yourself that will your friends amaze –
It's what you show of goodness all your days.

So stand up for the righteousness that peace and justice brings;
And value the rewards that give you greater wealth than kings;
And measure out true worth that sets the fires of love ablaze –
And seek to show your goodness;
Make the most of goodness;
Go and share your goodness all your days.

Twenty-fifth Sunday

Old Testament: Jeremiah 8:18-9:1
Epistle: 1 Timothy 2:1-7
Gospel: Luke 16:1-13

53 Riches

Doug couldn't wait for the start of the new football season. He'd been a United fanatic for as long as he could remember. He'd started going to games with his father and his grandad, in the days when little boys were passed over the turnstiles and had to be lifted up to sit on the crush-barriers to see anything of the game at all. When grandad died, Doug and his father continued their home-game ritual, and when watching football became all-seated, they had their regular places in the main stand with a familiar band of supporters round about.

His dad was a United season-ticket holder, and of course paid for his son's seat as well. It's what dads do, isn't it? In fact, Doug's dad did all the spending on the day of a game – the burger before the match, the half-time cola and crisps, the chocolate bar on the way home.

Doug looked forward to the time when he and his dad could do grown-up things together – over and above going to the game, that is, which always felt very grown up from those first over-the-turnstile days – like going to the pub on the way home, and Doug chipping in with his own funds, buying his dad a pint and a packet of crisps like two mates together. But the opportunity never arose. His dad died when Doug was seventeen. He never had the chance to buy the pints and packets of crisps and spend more quality time with his dad.

It took Doug some years to get back into the home-game routine. Oh, he'd gone to games, right enough. His mates had seen to that. Not every Saturday, though, because it wasn't the same without his dad. But this year was different. Doug was well into his apprentice-ship. He had money of his own. He'd saved hard since the start of the year, enough to buy his own season ticket ready for the beginning of the new season. It was the ultimate in growing up, the taking-up-of-the-torch as a United supporter which he'd pass on to his own son in later years, no doubt. Doug couldn't wait for the start of the new football season.

The opening league game didn't go well. United lost three-two to a debatable injury-time penalty. It was a bad day, so Doug chose to go straight home. He was too fed up for anything else. He hoped the rest of the season would be better than this.

It was on his way home that he read about Burkina Faso. It began with a poster in the bus shelter, encouraging people to donate to an emergency appeal for a drought-stricken country. Doug had no earthly clue where Burkina Faso was and he didn't like this kind of stuff in his face anyway, especially when he wasn't in the mood. So he didn't give it much thought, and busied himself reading the evening paper on the bus journey home. But Burkina Faso cropped up again, in a half-page advert in the newspaper from an international charity – West Africa, another failed harvest, heart-rending poverty, and much more besides. Doug pondered a home loss for United and the death of his father. He had enough troubles of his own, and so he turned to the next page of the evening paper to avoid the advert.

The evening news on TV brought it up again. Doug watched as aid workers cared for dying children and emaciated farmers walked forlornly through parched fields. Somehow a last minute dubious penalty at the first home game of the season didn't seem quite so important any more.

The harvest festival service at church the following day was the final straw. Doug wasn't a great church-goer, mostly confining his attendance to Christmas and weddings. But harvest festival was good fun. And his sister's kids would be there, singing lustily about apples and pears, wheat and bread, farmers and crops with the Sunday school choristers. And, blow me, didn't Burkina Faso turn up once more? Was someone trying to tell him something?

50p a day to secure meals all year round for families at risk of food shortages …

£25 a week towards distributing supplementary food to malnourished children and pregnant mothers …

£270 a month to support an agricultural worker to help sustain people's future livelihoods …

It was two weeks before Doug made a decision. In fact, it was on the way home after United's next home match. It had been a great day. United had beaten their arch-rivals two-nil. Riches beyond compare! Doug had felt very close to his father and his grandfather – and he'd been thinking a lot about the people of Burkina Faso too. He'd wondered if *they* ever had any good days …

That evening he set up a direct debit to an international relief organisation – for exactly the same amount as the monthly cost of his United season ticket.

Doug still enjoys his seat in United's main stand for all their home games. He still gets down when they lose or when he misses his dad. He still gets excited when they win and his dad is close to him again. He still has lots to enjoy. But now he knows that someone, some-where, on the other side of the world, who doesn't have many good days, who's experiencing grinding poverty and whom he's never likely to meet, might just have some kind of chance to grow up and have more hope of spending some quality time with their dad.

What?

What are riches?
What we have but did not earn …
What we own but did not create …
What we cherish but did not deserve …
What we value but did not achieve …

What is poverty?
What we need but do not find …
What we deserve but do not attain …

What we work for but do not receive ...
What we hope for but never fulfil ...

What is awareness?
What we see and choose to know ...
What we listen to and choose to hear ...
What we learn and choose to heed ...
What we feel and choose to understand ...

What is giving?
What we have and decide to share ...
What we own and decide to give away ...
What we cherish and decide to let go ...
What we value for ourselves and decide to value for others ...

Twenty-sixth Sunday

Old Testament: Jeremiah 32:1-3*a*, 6-15
Epistle: 1 Timothy 6:6-19
Gospel: Luke 16:19-31

54 Laurie Henderson's boat

Laurie Henderson was a boat-builder. He'd never worked in a ship-yard or a chandler's in his life, but he knew more about boats than anyone else in the village, and he was a boat-builder *par excellence*! It was model boats Laurie produced, each one better than the last. Laurie was a boat-builder right enough, and there was no one better.

Not for Laurie Henderson the plastic 'everything in the one kit' kind of boat-building. For Laurie, every single plank and railing, sail and rudder, was made by hand. Not for Laurie the battleship or cruiser, the ancient ship or flash speed-boat kind of boat-building. For Laurie it was fishing boats. Nothing else was worth bothering about.

Laurie had been a fisherman – in the days when there was a big fishing fleet based in his village. The sea was in his blood, as it had been for his father and grandfather and his three brothers. And now his two sons were at the fishing as well. And building model fishing boats had been handed down through the generations too.

Many of Laurie's best model boats adorned the windows of the streets around the harbour. There was the resplendent *Penelope Susan,* old Jake Ritchie's boat which had sadly been lost with all hands back in the 1940s. There was *The Charmer,* still to be seen in its full-size form plying the waters beyond the harbour, fishing for prawns and lobsters. There was the *Celtic Miracle,* reputedly named after the Glasgow Celtic football team who'd won the European Cup in 1967, though no one could remember any actual fishing boat which had carried that name. But no one bothered. They were just pleased that Laurie's boats continued to give so much pleasure to so many people.

By common agreement, Laurie Henderson's best ever boat was in the entrance foyer of the village Community Hall. *Valliant LH1950* had been Laurie's contribution to the refurbishment of the Commun-ity Hall after the war, offered in memory of those men from the village who'd been lost at sea during the conflict. There was no plaque on the shelf where the boat sat to say that, but Laurie knew what it meant.

The whole village was devastated when the Community Hall went on fire. In actual fact, the place was damaged more by smoke and the Fire Brigade's water than by the electrical fire that had caused the conflagration in the first place. Thankfully, *Valliant* survived, though it was clear that there would be a lot of cleaning and refurbishment required if the boat was to be restored to its original glory.

So it was a wet Wednesday afternoon when Laurie's granddaughter found a careful craftsman working on a big model boat on the kitchen table when she called in on her way home from school. 'Wot you up to Gramps?' she inquired. 'Playing table football with an invisible friend,' Laurie replied, not looking up from his work. 'C'mon, Gramps, be serious. What's this boat for, eh?' So granddaughter Katy got the whole story – the war, the seamen, the village, the Hall, the fire, the boat, the name, the registration number, the shelf for the boat in the foyer, the whole deal … 'Is LH after you, Gramps?' Katy asked. 'No, that's for Leith, where most of the boats from this village are registered.'

Katy loved her grandfather's stories, and, even more, loved to watch him work. So a skilled craftsman and an ardent admirer lapsed into silence for a while, as Katy watched her wonderful Gramps add the final small planks across the boat's forward hatchway. He put them in place and looked carefully. Then he took one away, skilfully filed an edge with a piece of glass-paper, and put it back again. He ran his finger across the miniature hatchway, but, still dissatisfied, expertly prised another tiny plank from its place, turned it around, and fitted it once more. Another stroke from a sensitive finger, a sideways look, a boat lifted to the light, a deep sigh, and Laurie Henderson pronounced himself satisfied.

Katy was transfixed. She thought the boat the most beautiful thing she had ever seen. But she was puzzled. 'Gramps,' she began, 'can I ask you a question?' 'You just did,' Laurie replied. 'C'mon Gramps, be serious. A real question …' 'Fire away,' an intrigued Laurie responded. 'Well,' Katy continued, 'why are you so careful with the little planks on the hatchway? No one's going to see them when *'Valliant'* is way up high on its shelf. Sure, they'll see the colours and the name, the rudder and the number. But no one's going to see the decking and the hatchways. So, why so careful? Why bother?'

Laurie smiled. He loved Katy's questions. 'Well, my lovely, it's like this. *I* need to know it's been done right.' 'But no one'll see it,' Katy insisted. 'Maybe not, but I'll know. I'll know it's right even if it's never seen by anyone ever again. What's hidden has to be right as well as what's seen. It's no good putting the best boat in the world on display if you know the hatchways aren't right.'

Katy was with Laurie and the family on the Sunday afternoon when the boat was returned to its rightful place on its shelf in the foyer of the village Community Hall. Everyone admired its glowing paintwork and the bright, white lettering of *'Valliant'* and *'LH1950'*. But Katy was thinking about the hatchways. She was pleased they were right too, even if no one could see them. And she was still thinking about hidden hatchways when she noticed her Gramps, Laurie Henderson, boat-builder *par excellence,* winking at her across the crowd gathered in the Community Hall foyer.

So small

God, I'm just a little boat,
and the ocean I sail in is so big …
Too many storms to face,
too many reefs to avoid,
too many rocks to navigate around.

I've got a good crew, though,
and I trust my captain absolutely.

33

But it doesn't stop me worrying
about being so small
when the seas around me are so huge.

But I've been well made,
and the spars and the sails and the rudder
are all top quality,
working well as they should,
doing their job for me.

And the little things are sorted too,
the things that no one else can see,
the hatchways and the ropes,
the galley and the bunks,
all in place, just as they should be.

God, I'm just a little boat,
and the ocean I sail in is so big …
But I'm well made, and I'm well crewed,
I'm well captained, and I'm well steered …
I may be small, but I'm in good hands.

Twenty-seventh Sunday

Old Testament: Lamentations 1:1–6
Epistle: 2 Timothy 1:1–14
Gospel: Luke 17:5–10

55 Just a wee note

The Callaghan family were notorious throughout the estate. Indeed, their fame had spread far beyond the bounds of the 1950s' housing area on the edge of the city. They were the talk of police-station canteens … Theirs was a familiar name on arrest warrants city-wide … They were a family of petty and serious criminals, and it had been that way for years.

Granny Callaghan was the matriarchal head of the Callaghan clan. A wizened old woman, retaining the strong Irish accent of her youth, she was a ken-speckled figure about the place and had lived in the same house for forty years. Granny Callaghan wasn't into criminality herself. She may have been the head of a notorious family, but she did not feel that this unfortunate notoriety should tarnish her own character.

Stan knew all about the Callaghan family. Well, as the curate in the local church you tend to pick up such information if you are willing to listen. Indeed, he knew Granny Callaghan well too, and she and Stan would often discuss all the troubles of the world – and the troubles of her family. 'I might see you at Mass on Sunday,' Stan would offer. 'You might or you might not,' Granny Callaghan would reply, 'for I have my own thoughts and don't need to come to Mass to sort those out.' 'Well, maybe someday,' was Stan's rejoinder, as another conversation came to an end.

Stan was distressed when he heard that Granny Callaghan's husband had died. A phone call with the local funeral director clarified the details of the funeral in the nearby cemetery, and, later in the day, Stan found himself at the Callaghans' sorting out the arrangements. There was a houseful! Much drink was being consumed. Much slinking off into the hallway and kitchen took place when Stan sat down beside the grieving widow. In time, the circumstances were clear and the arrangements were made. Stan had discovered that the old man had dropped dead in the garden and that the funeral would be attended by two sons from different prisons, and one grandson from a young offenders' institution.

That's why, at Myrtlehill cemetery later in the week, Stan conducted a funeral with the Callaghan clan gathered *en masse,* three prison-cars parked by the cemetery gate, three of the pallbearers holding their coffin-cord with one hand while the other was handcuffed to one of the prison-warders from three establishments of incarceration. Sad, verging on the awful, it certainly was, and after a brief conversation with her two sons and grandson, Granny Callaghan watched as the three men were returned to their respective places of confinement.

When Stan got news two weeks later that Granny Callaghan's third son had died in a tragic accident, he couldn't believe it. But true it certainly was, as Stan confirmed when he got the whole sorry tale from Granny Callaghan's own mouth. The son had apparently been prone to epilepsy, and, never good at taking his medication, he had taken a fit and fallen down the stairs. 'From awful to tragic,' Stan thought, and that was more than confirmed when the family gathered at Myrtlehill a few days later to lay a Callaghan son to rest. Again, the Callaghan clan … again, the three prison-cars … again the coffin being lowered with one hand with the other shackled to a warder, a coat or jacket covering the cuffs so that no one would know … But everyone knew, and when Granny Callaghan kissed goodbye to her sons and grandson, everyone knew where they were going back to.

A week later, Granny's Callaghan's sister was killed in a hit-and-run. 'From tragic to hellish …' was all Stan could think. Selfishly, he was thankful that this had happened on the other side of the country so he wasn't going to be involved. But he could picture the scene at another cemetery well enough - the Callaghan clan … the three prison-cars… the coffin being lowered with one hand, the other handcuffed … the farewell kiss … a devastated old Granny …

Stan decided he'd go to visit Granny Callaghan later that week.

The crowds had gone, the clan and their *entourage* had departed, and a wizened old woman sat alone by the fire. Stan offered her his hand. She took it and squeezed it hard. She looked up at the big curate and for the first time he saw the redness in her eyes. 'Thanks for coming, Stan, it means a lot.'

They talked for a bit, and as the conversation wore on Stan asked the obvious question. 'How are you coping with all of this?' 'Well, you just have to cope, don't you? I never asked for all of this to happen, and feeling sorry for myself won't make it go away. You live, you live. You die, you die. What can you do but make the best of things, eh?'

The following day Stan got home after a stressful day. Among the bills, circulars and junk-mail behind his front door, he found an old, opened envelope. The address on one side – Mrs B Callaghan - had been roughly scribbled out. And on the back, written in pencil, in a thin, spidery hand, he read:

'father stan this is just a wee note to say thanks for all youv dun for me and ma famly. your a good man and i'm glad youv come to see me. theres always an open door for you heer. thankyou. thankyou. Bridgette Callaghan.'

Stan's still got that letter. For he reckons that 'just a wee note ...' had given him the biggest 'thank you' ever.

Thank you

Thank you
For things achieved and purposes fulfilled.
Thank you
For caring given and tenderness expressed.
Thank you
For strength received and commitment enhanced.

Thank you
For comfort shared and peacefulness explored.
Thank you
For friendship found and confidence increased.
Thank you
For thank-yous given and gratitude received.
Thank you.

Twenty-eighth Sunday

Old Testament: Jeremiah 29:1, 4-7
Epistle: 2 Timothy 2:8-15
Gospel: Luke 17:11-19

56 Elvis gets a chance

The day of Elvis's appearance at the Sheriff Court had arrived. It had been a long time coming. Elvis – *aka* Andrew Wallace Burns Lenin Presley – had been languishing in Shortlane Remand Centre for weeks, and Martin, one of his ex-teachers, had visited regularly. Elvis, along with his older brother, had been arrested for theft of cigarettes from the local supermarket. But Martin loved the kid, for all of Elvis's obvious faults.

Martin had also popped in from time to time to see Elvis's mother. Mrs Presley was at home on her own and Martin had called in a few times to offer support. And when the day of her younger son's appearance in court came around, Martin took the morning off school and drove Mrs Presley to the Sheriff Court. They took their places at the back of the public benches. Elvis's mate, Terry, was there too. 'Ye huv tae support yer buddy, eh, Mr Miller?' Martin nodded.

As the morning wore on, much of the flotsam and jetsam of the town passed through the court. Martin was becoming singularly depressed as the hours went by. The Duty Court Solicitor had the responsibility of conducting Elvis's defence. He'd had a quiet word with Mrs Presley, muttered something by way of reassurance, and disappeared from the court to deal with other pressing matters.

Now, maybe it's because the flotsam and jetsam floated through the court quicker than the presiding Sheriff and his officials had expected … or perhaps the Sheriff was having a bad day and was disposing of cases more quickly and more severely than anyone was ready for … but, when it came Elvis's time to appear in the dock, the Duty Solicitor was nowhere to be seen.

There was restlessness in the well of the court. Elvis looked round, obviously confused. The Sheriff looked furious. 'Stand up, Mr Presley,' he barked at Elvis. 'Where's your solicitor? Why is he not here?'

'Don't know, sir,' came the tentative reply. 'What? Speak up?' retorted the irate Sheriff. 'Don't know where he is, sir,' Elvis continued, only slightly more audibly. The prosecuting lawyer stood up. 'He appears to have slipped out for a moment, m'lud,' he offered.

That was the final straw for the already distraught Mrs Presley at the back of the court. Her reaction could only be described as a wail. 'Oooohhh … Ma wee boy. It's no fair … He'll go doon … Oooohhh …' Everyone in the court turned round and stared, just in time to see Martin – distinctive as the only man in the public benches wearing a suit and collar and tie – put a big, comforting arm around the wailing Mrs Presley as she continued to sob uncontrollably.

The Sheriff, looking straight at Martin, barked, 'You there! Yes, you.' Martin looked up and hoped the Sheriff was shouting at someone else. No such luck! 'Yes you! Do you know this boy?' Before Martin could offer a response, the Sheriff crooked his finger and beckoned Martin forward. 'Approach the bench,' he ordered. Reluctantly, Martin did as he was bid and soon found himself face to face with the Sheriff.

'You know this boy?' 'Yes, I do,' Martin replied. 'In what way?' 'I was one of his teachers till he left school last summer, sir?' 'Do you know him well?' 'Yes, sir, very well indeed.' 'Tell me in one sentence what he is like.' Martin thought for a few seconds before replying. 'Well, sir, quite simply, he's a rogue – but a loveable one.' The Sheriff smiled for the first time that morning. 'Well, there's an honesty I don't often hear in this place. So, what should I do with your loveable rogue?' Martin took a deep breath and went for it … 'He's got a chance, sir, if you give him that chance today. He's got the offer to stay with his granny, away from trouble. His grandad reckons he can get him a job in the local garage. Elvis – sorry, Andrew – is up for that. But he won't have any chance if he goes down, or even if he's sucked into more trouble locally. He's a loveable rogue, right enough, but the loveable bit's worth working on.'

The Sheriff had stopped smiling and his stern countenance had returned. 'Step back,' he ordered. Martin returned quickly to his place in the public benches. 'Stand up, Mr Presley,' the Sheriff continued. 'I don't know why, but that man there thinks I should give you a chance. So ...' He paused for what seemed like an age. There was a hush in the court. Martin swore later that everyone was holding their breath. He had certainly been holding his. But eventually the silence was broken by the Sheriff's gruff voice. 'I am going to give you a sus-pended sentence ... three months ... suspended for two years ... but on this condition ... You will go to stay with your grandparents, and you will hold down a job. For if I have you back in front of me at *any* time in the future, Mr Presley, you will be for the high-jump. Do you understand?' Elvis nodded. 'Three months, suspended for two years. There's your chance. You're free to go.'

Outside the court, once reality had dawned for Mrs Presley, Terry and Martin, and when Elvis had been reunited with his support team, there was much back-slapping and rejoicing. Martin was clearly the hero. 'Mr Miller got Elvis off,' was what Terry spread round the estate later that day. But Martin knew the truth. A Sheriff had seen some potential in this kid, and, as a result, he'd given a loveable rogue a chance – a chance no one, least of all Elvis, ever thought he would have.

More thanks

Dear God

Thanks for today. I didn't think I would get another chance. To be honest, I'm not sure what I deserved after I'd blown it again. I don't know what you see in me or what makes you think I'm worth it. Maybe you see something in me that I don't see for myself.

Anyway, even though I don't really understand why you bother, I'm grateful that you do. So thanks for the chance to make another go of things.

I'll try to do better, honest. I hope it works out. If it doesn't, do you think another chance might be possible – just in case? Or is that pushing things too much?

Thanks for now – and for later too …

Yours sincerely

Tom

Twenty-ninth Sunday

Old Testament: Jeremiah 31:27-34
Epistle: 2 Timothy 3:14-4:5
Gospel: Luke 18:1-8

57 The showman preacher

Aggie Wilson was a regular at church. If fact, as far back as she could remember, going to church on a Sunday had been part of her life. And given the fact that she was now pushing eighty-seven, she had plenty of experience to draw upon.

The truth was … Aggie Wilson considered herself a bit of a form-critic of sermons. Preachers had come and gone, and, unbeknown to any one of them, Aggie had given each of them a score out of ten. One old preacher she remembered from her teenage years had never averaged more than two-and-a-half. One cracker, a visiting preacher from recent times, had got an eight. That was the best she could remember, better by a fair bit than the present incumbent in her local church who could occasionally rise to a six, but more often than not hovered around a four or a five.

The first Sunday in August there was a new visiting preacher, standing in, the congregation had been told, while the local chap was on his holidays. Aggie Wilson was in her usual place. She was full of expectation about the new man. She'd heard rumours of good things. So, when the preacher had mounted the pulpit steps and the time came for the sermon, Aggie Wilson was all ears. She was not to be disappointed.

The preacher surveyed the congregation without saying a word. It seemed like ages. The tension mounted. He closed his eyes tight. Aggie Wilson was bursting with anticipation. Then, the sermon began …

'My friends, people of God in this place,' the preacher intoned, 'I have to tell you this. I have been moved by the Spirit this day, MOVED BY THE SPIRIT, I SAY.' His voice was rising higher and higher. 'And the Spirit has told me that the sermon I had prepared for you today, I SHOULD NOT PREACH. The Spirit, my friends, has

given me ANOTHER WORD – ANOTHER WORD OF
TRUTH, I SAY, FOR THIS PEOPLE ON THIS GREAT DAY.'
And with a glorious flourish, he took the sheaf of notes he was
holding, tore them into little pieces, and threw them into the air. 'I
SHALL NOT PREACH THIS SERMON. THE SPIRIT HAS
GIVEN ME A NEW WORD FOR YOU, THE PEOPLE OF
GOD IN THIS PLACE!'

Aggie Wilson was *IMPRESSED*. The sermon itself would only
have scored a passable six. But with this attention-grabbing start, this
remarkable showman was up there with the best of them, and could
even have touched a nine-point-five.

When Aggie went to stay with her sister in the neighbouring
town a couple of weeks later, she told her the whole story of the
showman preacher. Imagine her delight, therefore, when her sister
informed her that this very man was to be the guest preacher at her
own church the following day. Aggie was excited, and by the time the
two old folk got to church on the Sunday morning, Aggie's sister was
up for it as well. In fact, altering the habit of a lifetime, they sat down
at the front, all the better to get the best from the showman preacher.

He didn't disappoint. When it came time for the sermon, the
preacher closed his eyes tight. Then, after a tension-inducing pause,
the sermon began ...

'My friends, people of God in this place,' the preacher intoned, 'I
have to tell you this. I have been moved by the Spirit this day,
MOVED BY THE SPIRIT, I SAY.' His voice was rising higher and
higher. 'And the Spirit has told me that the sermon I had prepared for
you today I SHOULD NOT PREACH. The Spirit, my friends, has
given me ANOTHER WORD – ANOTHER WORD OF
TRUTH, I SAY, FOR THIS PEOPLE ON THIS GREAT DAY.'
And with a glorious flourish, he took the sheaf of notes he was
holding, tore them into little pieces, and threw them into the air. 'I
SHALL NOT PREACH THIS SERMON. THE SPIRIT HAS
GIVEN ME A NEW WORD FOR YOU, THE PEOPLE OF GOD

IN THIS PLACE!'

Aggie Wilson was gob-smacked, and not at *all* impressed this time around - especially when the sermon was *exactly* the same as the one she'd heard in her own church two weeks before.

At the end of the service, while the congregation were filing out, Aggie held back for a bit, sneaked under the pulpit and gathered up some of the torn sermon notes the preacher had scattered around. On the way home on the bus she discovered that not one of them had a single word written on them. The preacher had torn up blank sheets of paper.

Aggie was tempted to become a preacher groupie, find out where the showman preacher had his next gig, see him go through what was clearly his standard opening routine, and stand up and shout 'YOU'RE A FRAUD! GO AWAY AND LEARN SOME HUMIL-ITY. YOU'RE NO MORE THAN A SHOWMAN.' But she con-tented herself simply by altering his score. The showman preacher was now averaging four-and-a-half, and that was *including* the atten-tion-grabbing opening.

Just as I am

'Just as I am,' I hear you say,
I should come close to you today.
And yet, mistakes get in the way,
Just as I am.

'Just as I am,' I hear your call,
Completely me, regrets and all,
Knowing how often I can fall,
Just as I am.

'Just I am,' I hear your plea,
Knowing your voice calls out to me;
This showman, down on bended knee,
Just as I am.

'Just as I am,' I hear my name;
I'm needed now, that is your claim,
Despite my overwhelming shame,
Just as I am.

'Just as I am,' I hear your word.
With me you will not be deterred
By what you've known and seen and heard,
Just as I am.

'Just as I am,' I hear your praise;
You will be with me all my days;
I'll know, through grace, forgiving ways,
Just as I am.

'Just as I am,' I hear you shout!
Come with your faith, and with your doubt.
This is what following is about –
Just as I am.

Thirtieth Sunday

Old Testament: Joel 2:23-32
Epistle: 2 Timothy 4:6-8, 16-18
Gospel: Luke 18:9-14

58 Knee-high

Knee-high hated his nickname. The label had been given to him by his grandfather. For it was clear, even when he was very young, that Knee-high was small for his age. 'Knee-high to a grasshopper,' grandfather had said – often! – and it had stuck. So all the way through school, Knee-high had to live with his hated nickname. Knee-high's real name was John Peter Livingstone. He was happy when he was plain Johnny Livingstone, but it was as JP Livingstone that he became more commonly known - and *that* was when his fame as a top-class jockey became more important than everything else.

It had begun when he was still in school, with a Saturday job in the racing stables in his Borders' town. He'd always had an interest in animals and horses were his first love. For as long as he could remember he'd had his mind set on being a vet and the job in the stables was an excellent beginning. But it was when he started riding that things took a different direction. He was a natural, and his ability even with the most difficult of horses was quickly recognised by the stables' top man, a trainer of a string of horses for local owners.

Johnny had become a stable-lad when he'd left school at sixteen, abandoning, for a time at least, his ambition to study at veterinary college. He'd learned the ropes riding out on the early-morning gallops. He'd become an apprentice jockey, and, at the age of seventeen, won his first race. From then on the name of JP Livingstone was to become familiar in racing circles, a by-word for riding skill and the potential for greatness. Being 'knee-high to a grasshopper' had become an asset, for JP Livingstone never had any problem 'making the weight' and keeping his small and wiry frame in good shape. Johnny knew that JP Livingstone's name was going to wipe out all of the hardships and connotations of being called 'Knee-high'. By the time he'd completed his apprenticeship he'd had dozens of winners.

He was a sensation in his first full season as a leading jockey. JP Livingstone couldn't fail.

It started to go wrong when the betting scandal hit the press. There had been rumours around for ages that some of the jockeys were 'on the take', linked to spread-betting irregularities in the Far East. Johnny had always been 'clean'. But when he was arrested along with five other jockeys and suspended 'pending the results of the enquiry', he was devastated. He sank into a depression. He began to drink more than was good for him. He lost control over his weight. And, worst of all, he wasn't allowed to ride or be associated with racing in any form.

Four of the six jockeys were found guilty of involvement with the betting scam. Johnny wasn't one of them. The case against him was dropped at an early stage. He came out of it all with an untarnished reputation - or at least that was the 'official' story. But the truth was that Johnny felt tainted by the whole affair, and his reputation was now questionable – 'guilt by association'. He was a broken man. All the old uncertainties came back to haunt him. JP Livingstone had gone. Knee-high had returned with all the self-doubt and low self-esteem of his youth. Vodka became a constant companion. Friends abandoned him. And riding for a living was a distant memory.

Johnny Livingstone doesn't know to this day why he chose to go to the evening race meeting at Kelso. After all, if racing had ostracised an innocent man so effectively, why would he want to have anything more to do with it ever again? But he just needed to be close to horses once more. Well, what did they know – or care – about tarnished reputations? And so, with his collar pulled up against the cold and his trilby pulled well down against possible recognition, Johnny Livingstone was leaning on the parade-ring rail watching the horses for the second race of the evening when a big arm appeared around his shoulders. Startled, Johnny pulled away from this unwelcome intrusion into his privacy. He looked around to see the source of the unexpected embrace, and found himself staring at the massive frame of Grenville Easington-Smyth.

'JP,' boomed Grenville cheerfully. 'Long time, no see, eh?' Grenville Easington-Smyth was one of the best known racehorse owners in the Borders. As a self-made millionaire through property development, for him horse racing was an enduring and indulgent passion and he owned a dozen or so good thoroughbreds. He was one of Johnny's favourite owners. 'I've been looking for you,' Grenville continued, 'and I'd been told you'd gone to ground since the enquiry.' Johnny looked up silently, not knowing how to respond. Grenville didn't seem to mind. 'Listen, JP, I've got a ride for you – Musselburgh – Sunday meeting – twelve furlongs – a race for two-year-old novices. I thought you'd appreciate the chance. If you can make the weight, the race is in five weeks. Fancy it?'

Johnny still didn't know what to say, but he smiled at the big man and nodded slowly. 'Good lad,' Grenville responded. 'You're far too good a jockey to let your talent go to waste. Come on, JP. Dinner's on me! I'll treat you to … a diet cola and a packet of low-fat crisps, eh? Making the weight starts now …' And with a big arm placed casually round Johnny's shoulders the two men went off towards the main stand.

Johnny smiled and this time he didn't pull away from the embrace. For at that moment he knew that Knee-high was being left behind again, and JP Livingstone was coming up fast on the stand-rail and might even win by a short head!

My name

You stop, and question if my birth
Brought forth a single thing of worth;
You wait, while all the world in mirth
Laughs me to shame;
You look, upwards from crowded earth,
And call my name.

I hope I will not meet your eyes,
And feel a fear within me rise;
I hide, and weep with silent cries
Of guilt and shame;
I'm done, as now I realise
You've called my name.

We touch, not knowing why or how
The future is beginning now;
We talk – and still my furrowed brow
Displays my shame;
We meet, the 'I' of me, the 'Thou'
Who knows my name.

I turn, and silently obey;
Unsure, and yet without delay;
I wonder if my eyes betray
More hidden shame …
I hope this is no judgement day
That sounds my name.

You say that you and I must go
To share my bread, that I might know
You will believe in me, and throw
Aside this shame.
You love – and in new birth I know
My blessèd name.

Thirty-first Sunday

Old Testament: Habakkuk 1:1-4; 2:1-4
Epistle: 2 Thessalonians. 1:1-4, 11-12
Gospel: Luke 19: 1-10

59 The old photo-frame

It was hard for Margaret to clear out Aunt Lizzie's house. It had been a home of welcome for her for many years, from her earliest memories of visiting the tenement flat at Christmas time with her family, to recent visits to a housebound, frail old lady.

Actually, Lizzie Paterson wasn't her aunt at all. She was, in fact, her grandfather's cousin, and Margaret had never figured out whether that made her a second cousin twice removed, or a great-aunt by marriage. Not that it mattered, because, for as long as she could remember, she'd been Margaret's Aunt Lizzie, and Aunt Lizzie had a home of love and welcome.

Aunt Lizzie had always been the kind of old aunt any young person would have dreamed of, and Margaret had loved her in a special way. When she was a precocious teenager she'd once asked Aunt Lizzie why she'd never married. The old lady had smiled and placed a finger to her lips to indicate that no more should be said. And that's the way it had remained, Lizzie Paterson's love-life never spoken of again.

Now that Lizzie Paterson was gone, the responsibility had fallen on Margaret's shoulders to break up her Aunt Lizzie's tenement home. It felt like an intrusion. As she moved dusty books from shelves into another sturdy cardboard box, Margaret felt she was handling personal things without permission. As she sorted through underwear and ornaments, well-thumbed Bibles and yet another packet of peach-scented soap, she felt she was intruding into private spaces that should be left unexplored. But it had to be done – and quickly. For the landlord wanted things cleared by the end of the month, and that was only two weeks away.

So, with a heavy heart, Margaret continued her painful and emotional chore. Sometimes she came across something that made her laugh – like the yellowed cutting from the local paper of Aunt Lizzie posing with the other ladies of the church Guild at the Easter Bonnet Parade of fifteen years before – with Lizzie Paterson as the winner. Sometimes she unearthed something that made her cry – like the birthday card signed by all the family for Aunt Lizzie's eightieth birthday just two years ago. And that's the way it was for the best part of a week as, slowly and carefully, Margaret sorted through more than eight decades of Lizzie Paterson's life.

She didn't think much of the brown-leather photo-frame when she found it behind the top row of paperbacks in the hall bookcase. It was old, that was for sure, and not in particularly good condition – another old artefact for the box of rubbish in the corner. And anyway, there was no photograph to stimulate Margaret's memory to laughter or tears. So she was about to toss the old frame aside when the back of it came loose in her hand. And, pulling it away from the frame, she was surprised to see an old photograph fluttering to the floor.

Laying the remains of the frame aside, Margaret bent down and retrieved the postcard-sized sepia picture. It was a photograph of a soldier in First World War uniform, posing, Victoriana-style, beside a large leather armchair. Forage-cap at a jaunty angle, this handsome young man wore the hint of a smile. 'Quite a lad,' thought Margaret, and wondered who it might be, for, as far as she knew, none of her family had served in the Great War.

Turning the old photograph over in her hand, she discovered a faint inscription written in a flowing hand on the back. The light in the hallway was poor and Margaret's eyesight wasn't what it was. So, retrieving her glasses from her handbag on the hall table, she made her way into the living room and, over by the widow, found the wording easier to decipher. 'To my darling Elizabeth,' it read. 'So far by distance – so close in our love. Wait for me, my beauty. Your only love, Joe. X X X'.

Again and again Margaret read the words, and the more she read, the more she wondered ... and the more she wondered, the more she cried ... and the more she cried, the more she smiled ... and the more she smiled, the more she thought she understood. Was this the reason why Lizzie Paterson had never married? Was this the reason why she was sure she'd seen something wistful in Aunt Lizzie's eyes at family weddings, at christening gatherings, at Christmas festivities? Was this the reason for the finger to the lips to silence a cheeky youngster? Joe ... 'Your only love ...' Never mentioned ... never spoken of ... just a hidden photograph in an old, leather frame, behind a row of paperback books ...

Carefully Margaret put the fragile photo back in the frame, but this time the picture of a handsome teenage soldier was smiling at her from the front and not hidden in the back. She found some tissue paper and, with the photo-frame carefully wrapped, she slipped it into her handbag with her glasses.

It was the only thing Margaret kept from her Aunt Lizzie's house. It was the only thing that seemed to matter. Now it sits on her sideboard, beside other photos of family events over the years. It has a picture of Aunt Lizzie as a young woman just beside it, the old photos of two happy young people, slightly turned towards each other. It seemed the right thing to do.

'Who's the good-looking soldier?' one of her friends enquired when she was visiting one day. 'Oh, that's Joe,' Margaret replied. 'He's an old family friend.'

What is love?

What is love
that it might be given
without condition,
with such commitment
that it changes my life?

It is love that lasts,
that stands the test of time,

which years or distance
cannot threaten
or destroy.

What is love
that it might be received
with full acceptance,
and celebration
and becomes all for me?

It is love that stays
and lives with your heart,
and keeps, forever new,
that which is mine to give
and yours to know.

What is Love
that it might make us one,
and bind us ever still
in what we give and take
in one true union?

It is the way to know
the truth that leads to life,
where love is ours
and fullness is our gift
that will not die with time.

All Saints

Old Testament: Daniel 7:1-3, 15-18
Epistle: Ephesians 1:11-23
Gospel: Luke 6:20-31

60 The clockmaker

Godfrey had been a clockmaker most of his life. Well, for most of his life there had been ample opportunity to work with skilled craftsmen in establishments where standards were high and clocks were made by hand. But with so many clocks being mass-produced or imported now, the demand for experienced clockmakers had declined. And with the advent of digital ... well, where was good workmanship any more?

So for the latter part of his working life Godfrey had been a watch- and clock-repairer in 'Good Chimes' at the end of the High Street. Sometimes a whole day would go by and all he'd done was replace watch batteries, or fit a new wrist strap, or sell a cheap digital watch. Once in a while he'd get a *proper* job to do – to repair a half-hunter fob-watch or restore the chimes in a mantelpiece clock. *That* was what his experience was for.

In time, arthritis in Godfrey's fingers put paid to even the most routine of tasks. He just didn't have the dexterity he needed. And when he had to give up for good, Godfrey missed making and repairing clocks. After all, it had been his life. He'd get excited when he saw an old clock on an antique or saleroom programme on the TV. But he missed being really involved.

When Godfrey's wife died and Social Services suggested he start attending the local day centre, he wasn't at all keen. He liked his own company, and even though he missed Jean an awful lot, he wasn't much for socialising. However, he was prepared to give it a try. It was as bad as he'd expected. Not that the people weren't nice – there were a couple of old guys who'd actually been quite friendly. But the men talked about football and Godfrey had never been into that. One of the women smelled of pee, so he kept well out of *her* way.

The week he'd decided it was going to be his last time, they had what they called 'a reminiscence session', talking about the old days and looking at photographs of what the town had been like before they'd pedestrianised the High Street. And there were pictures of things they'd used when they were young – a washing-board; a ration book from the Second World War; a spinning-top. They each had to say what the item was, suggest what it had been used for, guess how old it was, and tell a story about whether they'd come across it themselves.

Godfrey hadn't contributed much – even though he'd been familiar with just about everything. Until, that is, they'd shown the final picture. It was - a clock! 'What's that?' was the question. 'It's a grandfather clock,' someone replied. There were nods all round. 'How old do you think it is?' '100 years old?' came a suggestion. And then a pause, gently interrupted by Godfrey, offering, 'Actually, it's a Regency period longcase drum-head clock, probably made by Bryson of Edinburgh, around 1820 or so.'

There was a silence and everyone looked at Godfrey. 'Wow!' said one of the men. 'You're a dark horse, right enough. I'll bet that's not all you know, either, eh?' 'Would you be *interested* to hear some more?' Godfrey asked, his whispering voice barely concealing his apprehension. 'Yes, please!' almost everyone replied in chorus. 'Well, Robert Bryson was a clockmaker who had a shop in Princes Street in Edinburgh in the 1840s. He made a clock for the Royal Observatory round about that time. His sons, Alexander and Robert, continued the family firm, known as Robert Bryson & Sons, after their father died. This 13-inch silvered dial is typical of the period, with Roman numerals, twin winding holes, and matching steel hands. It'll have an eight-day movement and it'll strike on the hour. The case-work is probably mahogany, and I would reckon it's worth about £6000.'

There was a stunned silence – then, to Godfrey's surprise and embarrassment, a spontaneous round of applause. And that was the start of it. From then on, at some time of the day or another, the conversation with Godfrey would turn to clocks. Not that he hogged things, but sometimes people would test his expertise with pictures from books. One of the staff brought in an old mantel-clock one day so Godfrey could show the others how it was made and how it worked. Godfrey loved it, and the day centre became a lifeline for him.

One day, when people were gathering, Godfrey's seat was empty. 'Where's the old clockmaker?' one of the men asked. There were knowing looks among the staff. One of them came and sat in Godfrey's chair. 'Well ...' she began, and then stopped – for what seemed an awful long time. It was Tam who broke the silence. 'He's no' comin' back, is he?' Another long silence. 'Aye, ye cannae say it, lassie, but we ken fine. The old boy's dead, is that no' the truth?' A young staff member wiped away a tear and so did three old men. And another long silence held their collective sorrow.

Later in the morning when some normality had been restored, Godfrey's chair remained empty. Looking at it intently, Tam said, 'He was a nice old guy, wasn't he?' 'Aye, a fine man,' Henry replied, 'and there wasn't a bloody thing he didn't know about clocks.' 'But always modest with it,' Arthur continued. And that was the start of another reminiscence session – about drum-head grandfather clocks, and half-hunters, and eight-day movements, and clocks that chimed on the hour, and much more besides. But mostly it was about Godfrey, a clockmaker who was alive in their reminiscing even though his chair would never be filled again.

It's time

It's time, God said,
to think again of what has been,
and give your thanks for people and for places
who have touched your life with love.

It's time, dear God,
when thinking turns to prayer,

as thanks are given for places and for people
and the love they've left with me.

It's time, God said,
to think of what might be,
of hopes and dreams, and people and new places
who will offer life and love again.

It's time, dear God,
when hoping forms new prayers,
and dreams come true, and places and new people
give me all that's new, and right, and good.

Thirty-second Sunday

Old Testament: Haggai 1:14*b*-2:9
Epistle: 2 Thessalonians 2:1-5, 13-17
Gospel: Luke 20:27-38

61 Aunt Martha's flat

Tim never really enjoyed visiting Aunt Martha's. There was Uncle Joe there too, of course, because Aunt Martha and Uncle Joe lived together. But Aunt Martha, being clearly much more important than Uncle Joe, had the right to have the house named after her.

Aunt Martha's was on the other side of town, and Tim, his sister Carol and their parents went to visit Aunt Martha's every second Sunday. It took two buses to get there, so the trips there and home and the visit itself took up a whole afternoon. Tim never really enjoyed these visits.

It wasn't Aunt Martha that was the problem, even though she had some strange habits - like pouring her tea into her saucer to 'let it cool for a bit' (*very* odd indeed!). Uncle Joe was OK. He didn't say much, and just sat in the corner like another piece of furniture. Tim could even cope with the funny smell in the house, what he came to think of as 'Aunt Martha's smell', which he occasionally recognised when old people sat close to him on buses, or when mum took him to the old folks' home at Christmas.

Sitting still for ages was just about manageable ('Now, you *have* to behave, for Aunt Martha doesn't like fidgety boys.') And the watery orange juice and soft biscuits he and Carol politely had to endure were just about on the passable side. No, he could have coped reasonably well with all of that - if it wasn't for Aunt Martha's one-eyed cat.

Aunt Martha had a one-eyed, larger-than-life, ginger china cat which sat on the half-landing on the way up to her flat. It never moved. (Well, china cats don't, do they?) It just sat there, on guard, casting its beady eye over every person who came and went through Aunt Martha's front door and dared to set foot on her stair. And that one eye, suspiciously, critically, scarily, followed Tim as he slowly made his way past the ginger cat up to Aunt Martha's front room, sticking as close to the opposite wall as he could. And it followed him again as he left, even though he took great care to move a little quicker on the way out as he made his escape.

As far as Tim was aware, Aunt Martha's one-eyed cat had sat on the half-landing for ever and ever, or at least for as long as Aunt Martha had been around, and that, Tim reckoned, was a *very* long time indeed. He knew it wasn't a real cat, at least that's what his mum had reminded him of when he'd once told her he didn't like the beast. She'd laughed. 'Silly boy,' she'd said. 'It's a porcelain cat. It can't do you any harm.' 'That's as maybe,' Tim had thought, 'but the way that cat looks at me with his one eye tells me it could do all the harm it chooses.' There was no getting away from it … Tim didn't enjoy visiting Aunt Martha's because of her one-eyed ginger cat.

It was a bit of a problem, therefore, when Aunt Martha had to move house. Uncle Joe had to move with her too, of course, and couldn't be disposed of with the rest of the unneeded furniture. So, Tim heard his mum and dad say, it was 'sheltered housing' for them both, and closer to where Tim's family lived. He was *much* relieved. No more wasted Sunday afternoons. And … no more encounters with the one-eyed cat.

Tim wasn't at all chuffed when his mum and dad said they would have to visit Aunt Martha's again to 'see what needs to be moved'. It seemed as though Aunt Martha could take some things with her to the sheltered house, but not everything, because the new home was much smaller than the old flat. Tim scooted past the one-eyed cat as fast as he could – he reckoned he could at least run into Aunt Martha's flat because she wasn't there any more to be bothered about 'fidgety boys'. But the truth was, of course, that he needed to get past the one-eyed cat as quickly as possible.

He sat in the corner of the lounge while he watched his mum and dad talk, and point, and make lists. He followed them from room to room as they surveyed the whole flat, and obediently got his coat on when the work was done and it was time to go. He'd already decided he would run down the stairs and not even look at the one-eyed cat, leaving it behind for the very last time. Imagine his surprise, therefore, when, standing at the bottom of the stairs, he watched in horror as his mum picked up the one-eyed cat, put it under her arm, and carried it down the stairs. 'We'll have to take this,' she was saying to his dad. 'It's been around as long as Aunt Martha has. It can't *possibly* be left behind.'

The journey home on the bus with one-eyed cat perched on his mum's knee was hard to bear. And what was even worse was the one-eyed cat being placed in the hallway of his *own* home, just under where the coats hung, watching over everyone who came and went. 'Just temporarily ...' Tim's mother promised. But Tim wasn't so sure. This cat was *trouble*, and trouble wasn't going to be easy to escape. The one-eyed cat had it in for him, he was sure of that, and it looked like it was going to be *for ever* ...

Watching

Listen, God,
I need to get this clarified ...
Do you watch me all the time?
You know, if you're really 'omni-whatever',
like, everywhere at once,
do you watch me *all* the time?
It's not that I'm ashamed of anything –
well, at least not much ...
There *was* that incident on the bus to school yesterday
when I pinched one of Trudy's crisps when she wasn't looking
to get my own back for her writing on my school book
the day before.
I expect you saw *that* ...
I'm sorry, really I am,
and I promise I won't touch Trudy's crisps again,

unless she offers, of course,
(which she's not likely to) ...
But do you watch me in other places too,
like, when I'm changing,
or choosing my iPod tunes,
or watching my DVDs
or studying my maths
or washing my hair?
Does *that* really matter to you?
Shouldn't you be concentrating on more important things –
like Trudy writing on people's school books,
and the magazines my big brother buys,
and the war in Afghanistan?
I suppose I *know* you're 'omni-whatever',
like, everywhere at once,
or otherwise I wouldn't be talking to you like this,
now, would I?
But, can't you turn a blind eye,
well, just sometimes,
and focus on things that *really* matter
while I get on with changing
and watching TV?
I mean,
a person like me needs *some* moments of privacy,
even from an 'omni-whatever' kind of God,
don't you think?

Thirty-third Sunday

Old Testament: Isaiah 65:17-25
Epistle: 2 Thessalonians 3:6-13
Gospel: Luke 21:5-19

62 Andrew

Andrew was a fisherman. So were his four brothers, and their father. So were his three uncles, two of his brothers-in-law, three nephews, his next-door neighbour, and most of the other men in the village. So had been his grandfather and countless generations before that. And it was no different for almost every other family in the vicinity. Andrew was a fisherman, for that's what men did in every village down the coast.

Fishing was the life and livelihood for those who harvested the fruits of the ocean. It was the talk of the pubs. It was the economy of family life. It was the aspiration of the children. It was at the heart of everything. And it was the sustainer of faith, for there was not one family in the village who was not represented in one of the many local places of worship - mission halls, Brethren meeting houses, parish churches, Roman Catholic chapels. Sometimes even Andrew went to church, for the fleet never sailed on a Sunday, and no work was done repairing the boats or the nets on the day of rest. And when he didn't join the family for worship, he would join the other men down at the harbour, leaning on the rail, smoking his pipe, and talking about the fishing. For, above all else, Andrew was a fisherman.

And Andrew was a Saint. But, there again, so was almost everyone else in the area – man, woman and child. For that's what happened when you supported St Anthony FC in the local football league. Not that there wasn't support for the big city clubs. But the cities were far away and there were few opportunities to go to the big games, and even less inclination. So St Anthony's was the focus of everyone's interest – 'The Saints' of local affection and support.

The Saints were never very good, and it had been that way for generations. Nobody minded, least of all Andrew. But he'd played for them when he was young, and two of his nephews were regulars now.

So he was always interested, and, in between heated debates about the fishing, the fortunes of St Anthony's always figured somewhere.

St Anthony's FC had been the product, many years before, of a Roman Catholic mission to the area. But there was no partisanship now, and certainly no religious bias. You lived in the village, you had no choice, you supported St Anthony's – and, like every other St Anthony's supporter, that made you a Saint.

The young boy who slipped off the harbour wall one wet Sunday morning shouldn't have been there in the first place. He should have been in the mission hall with his mother and little sister. And he shouldn't have been stupid enough to be out at the end of the harbour bar in any event, not with such a wind blowing. But he wanted to fish, and the best fishing with his father's old rod was at the narrow entrance to the harbour. His father had always said so. And who worried about a bit of wind when there was fishing to be done? His father had always said so.

It was Andrew's brother who saw the lad slip and was the first to run to grab the lifebelt. Andrew was the first to respond to the shouts to the get boat out, and within minutes he and two others were turning the outboard round the end of the harbour wall and facing a running tide.

It wasn't a dramatic rescue. Andrew's brother was still in the water when they got to him with the outboard, hanging on to the metal ladder at the end of the harbour wall. The young lad was cradled in the lifebelt and a big fisherman's arm. It only took a few minutes to get a soaking man and an embarrassed teenager back to dry land and eventually to the warmth and safety of home.

It wasn't a dramatic event. It's what you do when you're a fisherman and you hear the call and somebody needs you. After all, it was Andrew's brother who got wet and did all the hard work. If there was a hero that wet Sunday morning, that's who it was. Andrew just did what he had to do.

It was back to the fishing for Andrew on the Monday morning.

264 A blessing to follow

He and the boys on the boat had a good week. All the Saints were home in time to watch St Anthony's win the following Saturday. The whole village was happy.

On the Sunday, Andrew didn't join the other men down at the harbour, leaning on the rail, smoking his pipe, and talking about the fishing or the football. Andrew, the Saint, went to the mission hall with his wife and he was delighted to see a young teenager there too with his mother and little sister.

Saints

Saints of then, to be admired and revered;
Saints of now, to be honoured and thanked.
Saints afar, to be shrouded in mystery;
Saints so near, to be seen, heard and touched.
Saints up there, to be lauded and sanctified;
Saints down here, to be copied and followed.
Saints of history, to be depicted in stained glass;
Saints of the present, to be freed to be themselves.
Saints in heaven, to be communing with each other;
Saints on earth, to be in communion with me.
Saints of fabulous stories, to be talked of again;
Saints alive, to be talked with right now.
Saints of plaster statues, to be looked up to;
Saints of flesh and blood, to be embraced in love.
Saints so holy, to be worshipped and adored;
Saints for me, to help me find my saintly potential.

St Andrew's Day – 30th November

Old Testament: Psalm 19:1-6
Epistle: Romans 10:8-18
Gospel: Matthew 4:18-22

63 A blessing to follow

'Are we there yet?' was a question Christopher's sister asked all the time. No sooner had dad turned the car out of the terrace where they lived onto the main road than Natalie would pipe up, 'Are we there yet?' Christopher and Natalie's mum was an expert in dealing with such a stupid question. Well, after all, it was a three-hour drive to Nan's and any fool knew that you couldn't *possibly* be 'there yet' after a minute and a half. But mum had methods for dealing with stupid questions from a little sister. It's what Christopher came to know later as 'distraction techniques' ...

There wasn't any point in starting a row and telling Natalie she was stupid and to stop asking such silly questions when the journey to Nan's had only just started. That would have just caused Natalie to go into a strop, and three hours of a little sister in a strop was more than *anyone* could bear, far less two parents and an older brother in the confined space of a family car on the way to Nan's.

On the other hand, Natalie was too little to understand explanations about distance and time. So there was no point in mum trying to be rational. Sensible explanations such as 'We've just left the house, so how can we be at Nan's yet?', or 'You've been to Nan's before, so you know it takes longer than that ...' would have been lost on such an irritating sister. But mum was clever, and so it was 'What song shall we sing while we are travelling?' or 'How many different colours of car can you see?' or 'Count the roundabouts ...' and suchlike. Distraction techniques a–plenty, three hours' worth, from a mum who was clearly an expert in such matters.

Of course Natalie would ask the question again from time to time: 'Are we there yet?' as they left the outskirts of their town, or joined the motorway, or pulled off for petrol, or even when they turned into Nan's road. It seemed obligatory for a small sister to be so irritating.

Christopher wondered if he'd ever asked 'Are we there yet?' or was as annoying or as silly as his sister. But, he figured, surely not …

Christopher, for as long as he could remember, had always loved the journey to Nan's. He'd been on the journey to Nan's lots and lots of times. Some family holidays were spent at Nan's. School mid-term breaks were inevitably spent at Nan's. And Christmases were *always* spent at Nan's. Christmas and going to Nan's went hand in hand. Christmas just wouldn't be the same anywhere else.

So Christopher knew what his little sister clearly had still to learn – that you could enjoy the journey to Nan's all the more if you knew what was waiting for you at the other end. He reckoned Natalie might get it one day, once she'd had a few more journeys under her belt. But Christopher had sussed it ages ago – that the journey was as important as the conclusion.

He knew all the times, and the landmarks, and the feelings of the journey. He knew the bits that were exciting, like driving past the massive football stadium of his favourite team, and dad telling the story again (and Christopher had heard it dozens of times before and still loved it) of the first big football match he'd ever gone to, and his grandad lifting him over the turnstile because little boys got in for nothing; he knew the parts he never liked, like having to wait in the traffic queue at the big roundabout not far from Nan's and feeling he hadn't moved for ages and *ages*; he knew times when it might be scary, like the time they'd had to drive through a *ginormous* thunderstorm, and he'd cried because he was frightened; he loved the times when he felt all cosy and warm, when he and mum were singing his favourite song, and mum would pretend to forget the words and Christopher would *always* get them right; he knew the time his mum would text Nan to let her know they were just about ten minutes away, and he could imagine his Nan getting the tea made and the juice and biscuits out to welcome them to her home; and, even now, when Natalie asked, 'Are we there yet?', and mum would be brilliant at distracting her all the way to Nan's, it seemed to have become part of the journey.

Christopher knew what Natalie had still to learn – that the journey was part of going to Nan's for Christmas, and being at Nan's for Christmas always made the journey worthwhile. Nothing could spoil that – not even huge thunderstorms or traffic jams or an irritating little sister. The end was always special. The journey took you there, and that made it worthwhile.

'Are we there yet?' was a question Christopher's sister asked all the time. No sooner had dad turned the car out of the terrace where they lived onto the main road than Natalie would pipe up, 'Are we there yet?' And Christopher would smile; because he knew that was the start of the journey, and at the end there would always be a blessing to follow.

★ ★ ★

A journey through the year, like Christopher's journey to his Nan's? Maybe …

So …

– What have been the landmarks on the journey?
– What have been the familiar stories that have benefited from being told and retold?
– Who have been the irritating sisters who still seem to be getting it wrong?
– Who are the comforting mums who make the journey worthwhile?
– When are the times you seem to be stuck, or the journey has been too slow?
– When are the times you've been scared?
– How are you sustained by the prospect of what is to come?
– How do you feel about the end of the journey?

The Roman philosopher Seneca wrote: 'Every new beginning comes from some other beginning's end.'

What new beginning waits for you at the end of a journey's beginning?

God of the journey

God of all new beginnings,
thank you for the promise of the journey.
God of familiar landmarks,
thank you for helpful signposts on the way.
God of real companionship,
thank you for stories of reassurance and love.
God of all the travellers,
help me be patient with those who still make mistakes.
God of saintly wisdom,
help me learn from those who are patient with me.
God of the journey's twists and turns,
help me to trust your strength when I am scared.
God of my weariness,
give me what I need to keep on going.
God of my anticipation,
give me the excitement of reaching the journey's end.
God of all my endings,
give me the hope I need at the end of the beginning.
God of all new beginnings,
thank you for your promise of our beginning again.

Final Sunday of the year

Old Testament: Jeremiah 23:1-6
Epistle: Colossians 1:11-20
Gospel: Luke 23:33-43

Also by Tom Gordon:

A Need for Living
Signposts on the journey of life and beyond
Everyone has a need for meaning in life. For most of us, it is only when we are facing a life crisis, or the loss of a loved one, or the reality of our own death that the search for meaning becomes real. How then do we express what really matters?

Facing this in his work as a hospice chaplain, Tom Gordon has often found that explanations sound trite and shallow, and even traditional beliefs can be found wanting. So, to help him understand and respond to people's search for meaning, he has come to use word pictures, imaginative concepts into which they can be drawn, and which can articulate their feelings better than words. This book contains a series of these images, woven together with some stories of people with whom they have been used.

It is a book for people facing a life crisis and for those who care for the dying. Ultimately it is for everyone, especially those for whom traditional words and symbols have failed, and who need new images to help them live again.

New Journeys Now Begin
Learning on the path of grief and loss
Bereavement is a journey to be travelled, not an illness to be treated or a problem to be solved. Tom Gordon writes with sensitivity and clarity about real people as they begin to understand their journeys of bereavement. He draws on his experience as a parish minister and hospice chaplain and his extensive involvement with bereavement support, as well as offering honest insights from his own journey of discovery. The book helps us understand the unplanned and often frightening twists and turns grief forces the bereaved to face.

The Iona Community is:

- An ecumenical movement of men and women from different walks of life and different traditions in the Christian church
- Committed to the gospel of Jesus Christ, and to following where that leads, even into the unknown
- Engaged together, and with people of goodwill across the world, in acting, reflecting and praying for justice, peace and the integrity of creation
- Convinced that the inclusive community we seek must be embodied in the community we practise

Together with our staff, we are responsible for:

- Our islands residential centres of Iona Abbey, the MacLeod Centre on Iona, and Camas Adventure Centre on the Ross of Mull

and in Glasgow:

- The administration of the Community
- Our work with young people
- Our publishing house, Wild Goose Publications
- Our association in the revitalising of worship with the Wild Goose Resource Group

The Iona Community was founded in Glasgow in 1938 by George MacLeod, minister, visionary and prophetic witness for peace, in the context of the poverty and despair of the Depression. Its original task of rebuilding the monastic ruins of Iona Abbey became a sign of hopeful rebuilding of community in Scotland and beyond. Today, we are about 250 Members, mostly in Britain, and 1500 Associate Members, with 1400 Friends worldwide. Together and apart, 'we follow the light we have, and pray for more light'.

For information on the Iona Community contact:
The Iona Community, Fourth Floor, Savoy House, 140 Sauchiehall Street, Glasgow G2 3DH, UK. Phone: 0141 332 6343
e-mail: admin@iona.org.uk; web: www.iona.org.uk

For enquiries about visiting Iona, please contact:
Iona Abbey, Isle of Iona, Argyll PA76 6SN, UK. Phone: 01681 700404
e-mail: ionacomm@iona.org.uk

Wild Goose Publications, the publishing house of the Iona Community established in the Celtic Christian tradition of Saint Columba, produces books, CDs and digital downloads on:

- holistic spirituality
- social justice
- political and peace issues
- healing
- innovative approaches to worship
- song in worship, including the work of the Wild Goose Resource Group
- material for meditation and reflection

For more information, please contact us at:

Wild Goose Publications
Fourth Floor, Savoy House
140 Sauchiehall Street,
Glasgow G2 3DH, UK

Tel. +44 (0)141 332 6292
Fax +44 (0)141 332 1090
e-mail: admin@ionabooks.com

or visit our website at
www.ionabooks.com
for details of all our products and online sales